C000153063

OH HAPPY COUNTRYMAN
A Suffolk Memoir

OTHER WORKS BY WILLIAM PAYN

*Ornamental Waterfowl — A Guide to their Care and Breeding.
Published by HF and G Witherby 1957 (reprinted 1968, 1974,
1979, 1986)*

*The Birds of Suffolk
Published by Barrie and Rockliff 1962 (2nd edition by Ancient
House Publishing 1978).*

With some of my birds at Hartest

OH HAPPY
COUNTRYMAN
A SUFFOLK MEMOIR

William H. Payn MBE, FLS, MBOU

The Book Guild Ltd.
Sussex, England

The Book Guild Ltd.
25 High Street,
Lewes, Sussex

First published 1994
Reprinted 1994
© William H. Payn 1994
Set in Times
Typesetting by Ashford Setting and Design Services
Ashford, Middlesex
Printed in Great Britain by
Antony Rowe Ltd.
Chippenham, Wiltshire.

A catalogue record for this book is available
from the British Library

ISBN 0 86332 933 0

CONTENTS

ACKNOWLEDGEMENTS

I am indebted to a number of Suffolk friends — mainly farmers, naturalists, conservationists, shooting folk and just plain countrymen and countrywomen, for valuable information, suggestions and comments for use in this memoir.

In particular I am grateful to John Wilson of Ixworth Thorpe, who has helped in many ways, including reading two of the chapters which cover his particular interests — conservation and shooting.

I am also most grateful to Benjamin Perkins who gave up so much of his valuable time to produce the admirable country scenes that illustrate each chapter.

Peter Hartley read and commented on the chapter describing the decrease in our farmland birds, a subject on which Philip Kerry, a life long naturalist friend from Hartest, has also commented most forcibly for years.

Robert Gooch, another countryman born and bred, has gone to great trouble, verbally and in writing, to convince me that farming practices are not necessarily harmful to our countryside.

I am grateful to Roger Clarke and M. R. Eke for providing photographs for the book jacket.

Michael Kelly has also helped in many ways, including sorting and selecting photographs, by suggesting appropriate words for the text when my own ideas had come to a dead end and for encouraging me throughout the whole operation.

Three ladies have dealt most efficiently, during various periods, with the typing of the manuscript. My thanks to them all.

Finally, I again offer thanks to the kind helpers listed below, some of whom have doubted whether this memoir would ever see the light of day; I am glad to show them that it has.

B J Brown
A L Bull
Mrs S Coleman
J G Darley (the late)
D Driver
R Eley
Mrs S Fisher
Mrs J Hawkins
Mrs S Hopwood
Miss A Lea
D R Moore
C R Naunton
F W Pawsey
M Rutterford
Mrs L Turner

INTRODUCTION

When my cousins and I were young our elders enjoyed regaling us with stories of their own childhoods in Suffolk. Among them was my maternal grandmother, born in 1862, and a most prolific teller of country tales.

We listened with polite interest, laughing when they were amusing and registering sorrow when they had an unhappy ending. Usually, within an hour or two the content of the stories and their details would have slithered off our little minds and been lost for ever. Nothing, so far as I know was ever committed to paper.

Innumerable family annecdotes have been lost in the same way during the passage of time.

Very few country people seem to have kept diaries, or even casual notes during the period when the countryside was changing so quickly. What jewels of social and, perhaps, historical interest have thus been lost to posterity.

I have kept diaries throughout most of my life. The first set, begun in 1927 while I was still at school, records natural history events and discoveries, and includes an account of peregrine falcons then nesting on the cliffs of the Avon Gorge. The account was later published in Country Life.

The second series of diaries covers such day to day events as I happen to note down and continues to this day to be useful for reference purposes.

The third set records my bird trips abroad, beginning in 1932 when I joined a collecting expedition to the Lebanon. It was the first, and the best remembered, of many such tours.

All three sets of diaries have provided material for this memoir.

History relates that when Charles II lay dying he apologised to those around him for the unconscionable time he was taking over it. Happily I am not in such pressing circumstances but feel, nevertheless, that I must apologise to those who have been awaiting publication of this memoir — I believe there are three or four of them — for the unconscionable time it has taken to get it between two covers.

The fault is all mine. I started it with enthusiasm, laboured on it for more than a year, became disheartened with its lack of progress and put it aside.

During this period I had to find time for a number of foreign bird watching tours — and inflicted on myself three house moves. The first move took me to the Channel Islands where, unaccountably, important material for the book was lost.

Each of the moves — the second brought me back after six years to my native Suffolk — involved me in the making, unmaking or remaking of a new garden. Enjoyment of a garden has long been on my list of life's joys.

Now that it is finished, I hope that those who read this memoir will find it interesting, and perhaps amusing. I have done my best to make it so.

Hartest   1993
Alderney, Channel Islands
Lawshall
Ixworth

1

MY COUNTRY FOREBEARS

As the time approaches when we must go to meet the old ferryman on the banks of the Styx, those of us who are not so young as we were tend, more and more, to retrace in memory our life's journey down the years.

We reflect on the things we have seen and done, on the people we have known. We ponder our achievements. Probably, most of all we meditate on the part played by good or ill-fortune as we have journeyed on our way.

Up to now — and I start this chronicle on my seventy-fifth birthday — my own journey has been marked by what was probably an average tally of joys and sorrows, of good and ill luck, but in one respect I know that I have been immeasurably blessed, in that I was born in the country and have been able to live there, in the same old house in the heart of Suffolk for the greater part of my life.

I come from a long line of countrymen and countrywomen. The first Payn of whom we have knowledge was Henry, who lived at Bourton-on-the-Water in Gloucestershire in the mid seventeenth century. He is said to have been a schoolmaster with two sons. One, Joseph, who died in 1742, had a son named James, the first of a number of James Payns. He too lived at Bourton-on-the-Water, where he married a local girl and combined the roles of schoolmaster and farmer.

His son, another James (1745-1822), climbed up in the world.

He lived at Kidwells in Berkshire, married Elizabeth Church of Maidenhead and became, in due course, county treasurer, Justice of the Peace and Mayor and Recorder of Maidenhead. I am told his portrait hangs in Maidenhead Town Hall.

This second James Payn's son, William (1770-1840) — he was the first William Payn, I look like being the last — followed his father as county treasurer. He married Harriet Moreland, daughter of William Moreland, master of the Old Berkshire Hounds. Though a Justice of the Peace for the County of Berkshire, William Payn is reputed to have been not only a fanatical sportsman, but also one of the greatest poachers of his time. In his gig, drawn by a very fast trotter and accompanied by a brace of pointers, he made lightning raids upon the partridge manors of Berkshire. Apparently he was never apprehended. As, occasionally, I have been called Poacher Payn by my more candid friends, I feel that the blood of Great-grandfather William must run strongly in my veins.

William had two sons, William the second, who became a major general and a Knight Commander of the Bath, and another James (1830-1898), who was my grandfather.

Though brought up in the country and in a very sporting family — his father also kept a pack of harriers — my grandfather is said to have hated all country sports and when sent out hunting would wait for a suitable opportunity, get off his pony, roll in the mud and then ride home saying he had had a bad fall and lost the hunt. At the age of eleven he was sent to Eton, which he also hated. From Eton, he was destined for the army and passed third into Woolwich but, after a year, his health gave way and his army career ended abruptly. Instead, he went up to Trinity College, Cambridge. I have here a blue and white plate from Trinity College which Grandfather appears to have purloined at some time.

On coming down from Cambridge he took up writing as a career and in due course became a very well-known Victorian novelist. He was also editor, at various times of The Cornhill, Chambers Journal and The Illustrated London News, and he had some one hundred novels to his credit. I must have most of them here, neatly bound in leather and gilt. They have good plots but are probably too leisurely and long winded for modern taste, though friends to whom I have lent them find them pleasant and amusing.

As author and editor James Payn became a close friend of many other authors of the period, among them Dickens, Trollope, Wilkie Collins and Thackeray, and he is said to have started Conan Doyle on his literary career. Anyone who may wish to know more about James Payn and his books should try to obtain a copy of his *The Backwater of Life*, a collection of quite delightful essays; also Victorian Popular Fiction, published by MacMillan.

Grandfather was married on his twenty-first birthday to Louisa Adelaide Edlin, daughter of a well-known Bond Street art dealer, and family legend avers that she was also the granddaughter of the Prince Regent, later King George IV. There are a number of pointers to the accuracy of this, but as nothing can now be proved, the matter is best forgotten. My grandparents had twelve children, of whom two were boys. My father was the youngest of them all.

Like the Payns, my mother's forebears were country born and bred, land owners, farmers and lawyers, with not a townsman among them. They were Hales and Goldings. The Goldings were a Suffolk family from Walsham-le-Willows. The Hales originated at Dauston (now spelt Dorstone) in Herefordshire, and the first of the clan, my great-great grandfather, Joseph Hale, came to live in Suffolk in 1763, when his parents bought him Somerton Hall on the occasion of his marriage to Miss Eaton of Stetchworth Park, Newmarket. Their son, Joseph Eaton Hale, married Sarah Forester Prosser, daughter of the Revd Thomas Prosser of Dauston. Previously she had been engaged to a man killed in a steeplechase. They had two sons, one of whom, Thomas Prosser Hale (1848-1897), was my grandfather. He married Ellen Isabel, daughter of Thomas Golding, a lawyer, of Walsham-le-Willows. Known as Old Bear by the family, Thomas Golding had built The Grove, a rather imposing house in Walsham, but he found it too expensive to maintain. so retired to The Bridge House, where he died.

As a very young child I was often taken to Bridge House where Thomas Golding's widow, who was a Miss Eckshaw from Kings County Ireland, still lived. She was, by then, totally blind and I well remember her being walked up and down the garden on the arm of her unmarried daughter, my Great-Aunt Angel. I also remember with equal clarity the superb apricots that grew on the garden wall and with which Aunt Angel — we always called her Aunt Jum for some forgotten reason — regaled me.

I can just remember Granny Payn, a small but determined watchdog in a lace cap, who trotted about the garden trying in vain to keep me out of mischief. I was told many little tales about her, most of which I have now forgotten, but I remember that on one occasion, while she was holding me on her lap, she fell off her chair and when asked whether she had injured herself, she is said to have replied: 'I think I have broken my thumb dear, but thank God I have saved the child'. She died in this house in 1917 and is buried at Somerton.

My other grandmother, Granny Hale, who lived to be ninety-one, was also small and very determined as most families' *mater familias* of the period seem to have been, used as they were to controlling a house full of children and domestics, and having to stand up to their more dominating spouses. Grandmother had been a most accomplished horsewoman and whip in her youth, going regularly to the Newmarket races and to many coursing meetings. She was particularly proud of her frequent mentions in *The Field* as the only lady to remain out throughout long and wet days' coursing.

Father's engagement to my mother very nearly foundered when, for a joke, he persuaded Granny Hale to fire a shot from his 12-bore gun. The recoil knocked her head over heels into the nearest ditch.

My maternal grandfather, Thomas Prosser Hale, must from all accounts have been a countryman in the truest sense of the word. A rich man with a passion for all forms of country activities and field sports, he owned most of the parishes of Somerton and Hawkedon, as well as Brook Hall, a large farm across the county boundary in Essex.

With little interest in business, he neglected his extensive farming interests, preferring to spend his time hunting, shooting, fishing and particularly hare coursing. He is said never to have had fewer than fifty greyhounds in his kennels at The Grove and at Somerton Hall. Sadly, though, he failed in his ambition to win the Waterloo Cup though he nominated Gallant the winner in 1897.

I have, hanging in my dining room, a large and rather attractive painting of a black and white greyhound by Edward Smythe. Grandmother always said that it was a painting of High Wind, one of grandfather's favourite dogs, but research undertaken by the keeper of the *Greyhound Studbook* confirms that High Wind was brindle in colour. The portrait is probably that of High Jinks, another of Grandfather's dogs.

Grandfather Hale was a paticularly fine whip renowned for the fact that he was regularly first off the course at Newmarket, after the royal carriages at the end of a day's racing.

Tommy Hale died at the age of forty-nine at the height of the agricultural slump, and Grandmother was left with three little daughters to bring up. Her advisers recommended the sale of the entire estate and this duly took place when some of the best Suffolk cornland was selling for only £3 or £4 an acre. To add insult to injury a good deal of the land was bought by Grandfather's ex-bailiff with, it was always said, Hale money which had found its way irregularly into the bailiff's pocket.

When, as a child, I drove with my father about the Suffolk lanes and we passed the person concerned — he was an odd looking old man who always wore a dirty old solar topee — Father would point to him and say: 'There, my boy, goes most of your Hale family money.'

The above remark brings my dear father into the picture. He was educated privately, qualified as a naval engineer and worked for some years at the Thomas Ironworks where he used to tell me, he helped design the last ironclad warship built on the Thames. It was, I think, built for the Japanese navy.

Never very strong, Father was warned at the age of twenty-two that he must not continue to live and work in a city.

As a result he moved to Suffolk. I am not clear why my

father was originally attracted to Suffolk. He certainly had shooting friends here and used to tell me that he often travelled down by train from London for a day's shooting. At that time he also did a lot of wildfowling both on the Thames and at Mersea Island on the River Blackwater. Somewhere I have an article he wrote for *Land and Water* about a wildfowling holiday at Mersea.

Whatever the reason, he had become so fond of Suffolk that on being told he must no longer live in London, he rented as a shooting-box Manor Farm, Somerton, which is only some half-mile across the fields from the house in which I am now writing, and which was later to become his home for twenty-five years. There, at Manor Farm, he lived the life of a country gentleman, shooting, fishing and entertaining his friends. Many years later I rented the shooting on Manor Farm myself.

At Manor Farm, my father was looked after by the farmer's wife. Unfortunately, this arrangement did not always work smoothly as the good lady, whom I will call Mrs D, suffered from depression — cured only by frequent recourse to the gin bottle. In this connection Father used to amuse us with two little stories. On one occasion he had invited some of his local friends to supper and, in consultation with Mrs D, it had been arranged that the fare should consist of roast goose and gooseberry pie — indeed, Mrs D's gooseberry pies were famous. Unhappily, on the evening in question, Mrs D was not at her best and Father had his misgivings. The goose looked all right when it arrived on the table but, the moment he inserted the carving knife the bird crumbled to pieces having been cooked to a crisp. The hopes of the party were, however, buoyed up at the prospect of the famous gooseberry pie, only to be dashed a little later when, on entering the room bearing aloft her delectable dish, Mrs D caught her toe on the threshold and the pie shot into the room ending in fragments on the floor. The assembled company had to make do with bread and cheese and, I hope, a good bottle of port.

A pudding again featured prominently in the second incident. Father had invited friends to supper and asked Mrs D to prvide a large suet pudding. Unfortunately things had not gone well in the kitchen and when it arrived the pudding proved far too heavy and solid for human consumption. What was to be done? Mrs D's feelings must, on no account, be hurt. Then Father had a happy idea. It being quite dark, he crept out into the stable yard and dropped the pudding into the duck pond, confident that by morning it would have sunk without trace or, more probably, been eaten by the ducks.

But an early morning reconnaissance revealed the awful presence of the pudding bobbing in full view in the middle of the pond. Drastic action was called for. Father fetched his gun and blew the pudding to smithereens.

As he no longer had a London base, and the Manor Farm regime was not entirely satisfactory, Father later bought a small house in the adjoining village of Hawkedon, where he installed himself with his old governess as housekeeper, and settled down to the life of a country gentleman.

He soon acquired a wide circle of friends, among them the Poleys of Boxted Hall and the Hales of Somerton Hall. The Hales had three daughters, one of whom, Eileen, was to become my mother.

2

EARLY DAYS

I was just six months old when my parents brought me to live in this dear old house which has been my home now for close on seventy years. Naturally I remember very little of my early years here, but as memory gropes back it brings stray fragments of scenes or events from the recesses of my mind.

The first fragment that comes to mind — and it is a very important one — conjures up something that took place in the spring of 1917. My father's first cousin Colonel Arthur Payn, had been invalided home from the Front suffering from wounds and shellshock, and had come to recuperate at Hartest. He was a dedicated naturalist and I can well remember him lifting me up to look into a song thrush's nest in an ilex tree in the shrubbery here. The tree is still standing and I can recall the intense thrill that went through me as I beheld those blue, black-freckled eggs, gleaming against the clay lining of the nest. I was enchanted. I was four years old and the little episode, which I can recall as clearly as if it had happened yesterday, marked the beginning of a passion for birds and other wild creatures which has dominated my life ever since.

My infancy was framed almost exactly within the years of the Great War (1914-18), from which memory produces another fragment, this time of being taken out into the garden at night to listen to the throb of engines in the sky overhead — the engines of a Zeppelin. It was the same craft which was shot down later that night at Cuffley in Hertfordshire. Could I have seen its lights as it passed over us, as I also seem to remember?

I certainly do remember the fat airships, called Pulham Hogs, which flew regularly over our house from their base at Pulham in Norfolk. I recollect, too, my mother and nurse taking me to the seaside at Felixstowe, a visit which left me with a clear mental picture of soldiers being drilled daily by an officer with a shrill voice, whom we unkindly christened Aunt Jane.

One other event connected with that war is enshrined in our family annals. In the summer of 1914 my cousin, George Buckle, son of G E Buckle, editor of *'The Times'*, was staying with us at Hartest. On the fourth of August he was playing cricket for the Hartest village team on the meadow just beyond the garden, when news was brought to Father that Britain had declared war on Germany. I was too young to comprehend anything of the events of that war, but should see my share of the next one.

Besides my parents and myself, our household at that time was quite large by modern standards, though not unusual for the period when the pound was still worth twenty shillings and a shilling would buy a good deal.

Outside in the garden was old Mr Pettit and a garden boy, both firm allies of mine, while a cook and a parlourmaid coped with our domestic needs indoors. There was also a series of nannies, each uniformed in linen cap and apron, whose main occupations, judging by such photographs as have survived, seem to have consisted of pushing me about in my pram or in a small wheelbarrow, and clinging firmly to my sashes whilst I hung head downwards to inspect the denizens of the front pond.

Those nannies survived until I was packed off to a boarding school at Hove, at the tender age of six. Was I by that time too much of a handful for a mere nanny? One, with whom I am still in close touch, says I was 'a proper little demon', which I don't doubt for one moment. Indeed knowing my own character and mental processes, I can guess that long before I was released from my nannies' apron strings, I had explored every inch of the house and garden and their surroundings, and was becoming acquainted with much of the fascinating wildlife to be found then in the Suffolk countryside.

As the slow seasons of my childhood succeeded each other and I grew bigger and still more enterprising, the range of my activities widened. By the time I was seven or eight I was ranging far and wide over the four parishes which encompassed my home. Encouraged by my parents and two naturalist cousins, I became an avid collector of birds' eggs and butterflies, the classic start for all naturalists in those days.

Most estate owners and farmers over whose land I roamed knew Father well — as did their gamekeepers, so usually I was left in peace to go where I liked in my search for birds and butterflies. Those who owned or worked on the land then were sympathetic to such activities, for countrymen in those days lived closer to nature and took more interest in it than is generally the case today, when so much of the wildlife of the farms has been destroyed.

So, wandering alone with only the family dog for company — for I was a solitary child — I became acquainted with most of the ponds and marshes, the woods and areas of wasteland in the neighbourhood, and knew what birds and beasts and butterflies were to be found in them.

Each season of the year provided new scope for my activities. The Easter holidays were given over to birds' nesting and to accompanying my father's gamekeeper, little William Hunt, on his daily rounds. From him I learned much of my country lore and of the ways of bird and beast. Already I knew where to look for the nests of the many pairs of snipe that returned season after season to nest in the water meadows in the valley or in some small boggy patch, often no more than half an acre in extent, which was then to be found on most farms within easy walking distance of my home.

Each April the thrill was renewed as I looked down upon another nest with its four green and chocolate eggs, lying neatly arranged, points inwards, in their nesting hollow amid the rushes, while the cock bird sang his curious 'chipper chipper chipper' cadence as he soared and swooped overhead, ending with that wonderful aerial bleating which always sends a tingle down my spine. Now all those bogs and water meadows are barley fields, and the nesting snipe have gone for ever.

In the summer, when days and weeks never seemed long enough for all the things I wanted to do, I was always on the go, busy with some outdoor activity. I spent hours fishing for carp and roach in the local ponds, particularly in the pond at Brockely Rectory which contained some — to me — monster carp which, when captured, were brought home in triumph and released in the front pond in the garden here.

When the weather served, it was all moth and butterfly hunting. I painted the trunks of the orchard trees with a mixture of beer, treacle and pear essence — the process known as sugaring to attract desirable moths, or scoured the lanes and clover fields for butterflies, particularly for such exciting strangers as painted ladies and the handsome orange and black clouded yellows, which only appeared in really hot summers.

In such summers, too, I enjoyed bathing in my own secret pool in the river at Somerton; it had deep water and a sandy bottom and was far from prying eyes. In it I also taught several generations of Labrador pups how to swim and retrieve from water.

All these activities had somehow to be fitted in to allow me time in the harvest fields when the corn was being cut in August.

The Suffolk harvest field, as I first remember it more than half a century ago, was a far more interesting and colourful place than it has since become. My mind's eye recalls the scene as though it were yesterday: the sun is shining on a field of rippling wheat, framed against a background of tall elms and tall hedges. Part of the field has already been harvested and the binder, its sails whirling, continues round and round, reducing by a swathe at each circuit the area of corn still uncut. Its two great chestnut horses — they are of course 'Suffolk Punches' — plod steadily round with an occasional snort or toss of the head, for the flies are troublesome, despite the green leaves tucked for protection into their bridles.

The two men on the machine are alert and vigilant, the driver must watch his horses, though probably they know their job as well as he, and must keep an eye on the movement of the blades as they shuttle to and fro in the cutter bar; his mate, up behind, watches the mechanism that bundles and ties the corn into sheaves before ejecting them sideways on to the stubble.

So, round and round they go, men and beasts in harmony, circuit after circuit, sometimes all day long if it is a large field, while overhead the swallows swoop and dart for they, too, have a harvest to garner, the harvest of insects disturbed from the tumbling corn.

Soon after the binder starts other men move on to the field to set the fallen sheaves up into shocks — we called them shocks in Suffolk, never stooks — to await haulage to the farmyard. In those days the sheaves were propped against each other, head to head: if wheat, there were four or six a side to each shock; if barley there could be any number a side, but oats had only four sheaves on each side of the shock and good farmers always said that oats must stand for three Sundays in the shock before being carted.

Rabbits were very numerous then on most Suffolk farms and their meat was popular in village homes, our own included. When it was known that a corn field likely to contain a good number of rabbits was nearing completion, a cavalcade of small boys on foot or on cycles, and all armed with sticks longer than themselves, would converge on the scene, eager for some sport and the chance of taking home a rabbit or two for the pot. Usually I was among them, supported by my faithful shadow, Trick.

The gamekeeper and the farmer were there also with their guns, the former to see that his pheasants and partridges were allowed to escape unscathed from the blades of the reaper and — if his master were not a hunting man — to deal with any fox that might try to slink away. The farmer would have been hoping to get a hare for his dinner.

If it were a fine day, and the field lay near the village the whole thing was turned into a social occasion; the women took their small children to play among the sheaves, and holiday visitors and even, sometimes, the village policeman, went to gossip and watch proceedings. It became a happy occasion for all, except, of course, for the rabbits. Modern farming methods, huge fields and a marked decrease in the rabbit population has put an end to such rural amusements.

Come September, and with harvest safely gathered, my interest centred on Father's partridge shoots, the highlights of my summer holidays, when I was allowed to take part with my little gun.

Then back to school and three arid, wasted months dragged slowly by till the Christmas holidays came round and there were pheasant-shooting days and often the excitement of snow and frost. Each winter our village seemed to be snowed-up at least once, with great drifts filling the roads and lanes till they were level with the hedges, and men had to set to with spades to dig a way through to isolated farms and to clear the roads for the mail. Then, as I dashed out in the morning to a world transformed overnight into a white wasteland, my imagination allowed me to think of myself as the first man in the Moon or an explorer nearing the North Pole.

There was also the fun of being the first to leave footprints on some great sheet of snow into which one might disappear up to the shoulders when a drift suddenly gave way.

A fresh fall of snow provided yet another interest for the ardent naturalist and hunter that I was fast becoming; the white surface was a page upon which the night prowlers wrote an account of what they did and where they went while the human world was asleep. Round the outbuildings I learned whether we had rats that needed trapping and whether unwelcome cats were invading the garden at night.

The meadows outside were always criss-crossed by innumerable hare and rabbit tracks, and those of an occasional stoat, while sometimes I could pick out the neat, pointed footprints of a prowling fox. This gave a chance to test my field craft as I followed its devious roamings over hedge and ditch and through tangled spinneys. I was always learning.

After the snow came great frosts to grip the land. Within a few days every pond and stream was frozen over, providing more thrills. No country child could resist sliding on the ice and sometimes did so before it was safe, even though we all knew the old saying about frozen ponds that 'cracks she bears, bend she breaks' When, once, I ignored that good country saw

24

it could have ended in disaster. Three or four small boys from the village, and I, were preparing to slide on a deep pond away in the fields. Bolder, or more rash than the rest, I ventured out alone to test the ice, even though it was tending to bend under my light weight. A moment later I was struggling up to my shoulders in bitterly cold water. My companions made no attempt to rescue me but with one accord dashed off to their homes to report that 'Master William was drowning'. Help would, of course, have arrived far too late. Somehow I managed to claw my way through the ice and scramble ashore; cold, dripping and slightly wiser, I staggered home to a hot bath and a severe wigging from my mama. It was the first of many of my lucky escapes.

One activity which helped to enliven the winter months on every farm, and which was eagerly anticipated by small boys, was the arrival of the thrashing tackle. Hauled by a steam engine with a brass badge of a rearing horse on the front of its boiler, the tackle consisted of a long train of implements including the red painted thrashing drum, the elevator for dealing with the straw, a water cart, coal cart and other impedimenta. The equipment was accompanied by a team of three or four men who travelled about with it from farm to farm.

In those days every Suffolk farm had a permanent stack yard which was used year after year, and which contained a number of iron structures, circular or oblong in shape, and raised about three feet from the ground on mushroom shaped supports of iron or stone. Known as staddle stones, they were designed to keep the stack dry and to prevent rats and mice climbing up into it. On each of these frames a stack was built up straight from the loaded wagons as the corn was brought in from the harvest field in autumn.

On some of the larger farms twenty or more great stacks were put up in a few weeks. Each had a steeply pitched roof, thatched by either a professional thatcher, or by a farmworker, to keep out the weather. The thatch, of the best wheat straw, was held down by sharpened pegs made of split hazel and known as 'brorches', the making of which was a skill in itself.

With the arrival of the thrashing tackle, the stack yard became a hive of activity; the engine, straw elevator and the thrashing drum were positioned alongside the first stack to be thrashed, piles of great jute sacks were brought from the barns, the coal cart and water cart were stationed nearby and ladders were propped up against the stack. Two or three of the farm workers then mounted aloft and, armed with pitchforks, set about stripping off the thatch.

With steam up on the engine, the pulley belt between it and the thrashing drum began to turn and as a steady flow of sheaves was forked down by the men on the stack, the thrashing drum burst into life with a merry hum and operations were under way. It was an animated scene; of the three men on top of the stack two were kept busy forking down the sheaves into the drum, amid a cloud of dust and debris, while the third had the worst job as he had to cut the twine that bound the sheaves before they went into the drum, and his hair and clothes were soon full of dust, chaff, barley awns, and other debris from the stack. Down below, the drum shook and hummed, vibrating with the effort of winnowing the grain from the straw which was carried away by the elevator to be built up into a stack closeby.

The grain, meanwhile, cascaded out of a number of spouts at one end of the drum into the great sacks hanging there to catch it, while the small waste corn, called tailings, poured out from another spout.

As each stack was steadily reduced in height until it was no more than about seven or eight feet, the rats and mice that had been living there in warmth and plenty throughout the winter began to run out in all directions. This was the moment for which we boys, with our attendant dogs, had been waiting so eagerly. With sticks and stamping feet we tried to intercept every rat or mouse that came dashing out as the last sheaves were lifted up; at times the last two or three feet of a stack would absolutely heave with the number of rats and mice still trapped within it. The slaughter by snapping dogs and flailing sticks was often considerable and few rats managed to escape. My dog Trick and I joined in with the greatest enthusiasm but I always watched out for, and tried to protect, the beautiful and harmless little harvest mice. Very small and brilliant

26

orange-yellow, they showed up like small streaks of fire as they made their dash for freedom across the straw. Now that the combine harvester has taken the place of the thrashing machine, such lively scenes have become things of the past.

So the years of my early childhood sped swiftly by, with me immersed in the events and activities of the countryside about my home. I was immeasurably happy in my way of life, yet I suppose the modern boy with his television and radio, his easy mobility by car and plane and his sophisticated toys and organised games — all of which he takes for granted — would consider my life then to have been primitive and lacking in excitement and interest. I would happily return to those far off days. Life in a Suffolk village when I was a child was so different from what it is today that I sometimes wonder, as I look back on it all, whether I can really be thinking of the same part of the universe.

We lived then in a far smaller and slower world in which each village was largely self-sufficient, relying for most of its basic needs on its own efforts and skills without being dependent, as we all are now, on such conveniences as electricity and mains water, over the provision of which we have no control whatever.

The village community was the centre of life, providing work of some sort for the majority of its inhabitants as well as most of their amusements and recreations. The economy of the village was based on its farms. In Hartest, there were at that time some ten farms each of about one hundred acres in extent, which was about the average size for the neighbourhood. Each farm gave full time employment to at least three men and the odd boy. Others worked in the shops or were skilled craftsmen such as carpenters, thatchers and bricklayers. Most of the girls went into domestic service at the larger farms and private houses in the neighbourhood as soon as they left school, and those houses and farms also employed some of the men as gardeners or grooms. Those who worked in the village seldom lived more than a few miles away.

With some four hundred inhabitants, Hartest was one of the larger villages in the neighbourhood, big enough to provide a living for three bakeries, one of which — Ellinghams — kept cream coloured horses to pull the delivery vans; I can clearly recall those handsome horses grazing in summer on the village green. We also had two butchers, a small sweet shop, a cobblers, always known in the Suffolk dialect as 'the shimmaker', two general builders, one of whom made coffins — and centres of daily gossip and activity, Crickmore and Savage's grocery, which also sold clothing, and the post office, presided over by two great village characters, old Mrs Redgrave and her daughter Ethel.

There was also the blacksmith, who played an imprtant part in the village economy for he shod the farm and carriage horses, repaired machinery and made all kinds of ironwork, including the vital iron tyres for the wagon wheels.

No true countryman could ever pass a blacksmith's forge without dallying to watch proceedings within, and I was no exception. The forge was almost as important a social centre as the village pub. The building seemed always to be in semi-darkness for its only window was usually festooned with cobwebs and odd bits of ironwork, whilst such light as came through the open doorway was often half obscured by a bystander or two, or by a horse waiting its turn to be shod. Within, the smith was to be seen leaning over his glowing forge, the firelight illuminating his face and bare arms and the heavy leather apron which covered him from neck to ankles. He seemed to be for ever clanging away at some piece of red hot iron, while his mate worked the great leather bellows which kept the fire glowing.

I particularly enjoyed looking on while Mr Rawlings, our blacksmith, was shoeing a farm horse. A collection of roughly shaped iron shoes was always kept hanging from a rack on the wall. From these the smith selected one he thought suitable and, while the horse's attendant held its head, he lifted up each great foot, resting it on his knee and trying the rough shoe for size and shape; a new shoe must fit exactly or the horse would quickly go lame. Then the selected shoe was taken back to the fire and held with long-handled tongs within the glowing coals till, with the bellows going full blast amid showers of sparks, the iron turned red and then white hot. Next, the glowing iron was carried back to the anvil and beaten into the required shape with holes for the nails deftly punched through it before the whole thing was plunged into a tank of water to cool amid clouds of steam.

With a sharp knife the smith had already trimmed the inside of the hoof and, while the shoe was still hot, it was clamped on to the hoof and nailed into place while the air was filled with the smell of burning horn. Some horses disliked being shod and gave trouble but most seemed to take the whole operation as a matter of course. Nowadays there are very few general blacksmiths left in the villages and those who survive prefer to call themselves agricultural engineers.

Domestic arrangements in the villages were somewhat backward. Most houses were dependent on earth closets at the end of the garden and, with piped water almost unknown, people drew their drinking water from wells which were centuries old and which frequently went dry. Washing water came from water butts or even from ponds. On Hartest Green there were two hand pumps maintained by the parish council, and many houses had their own wells. Ours was a very deep bore which went down into the chalk and the gardener and his boy spent two hours every day pumping the water by hand into storage tanks in the attic. Later the hand pump was replaced by an 'Indian' paraffin engine.

Tom Cornish, the thatcher, and his family, who lived just up the road, caught all their drinking water in a bucket placed below a field drain. They all lived to a ripe old age.

At Hawkedon, where I stayed regularly at Rose Cottage with Father's old governess, the best well was situated just outside the churchyard wall. Its water was crystal clear and fresh, unlike the flat tasteless stuff that now comes from our pipes. I remember that the well usually contained a frog or two and small boys amused themselves by dropping live minnows and sticklebacks into it. Nobody seemed to mind.

In those blissful days there was very little traffic on the country roads and nearly all of it was horse drawn; farmers still rode on horseback or in dog carts and traps, and the great creaking wagons and two-wheeled tumbrils in use on the farms were also about on the roads with their loads of grain, faggots or manure. There were a few wagonettes — four-wheeled open carriages capable of holding six or eight people — and small governess carts. If one hadn't a horse or that rarity, a motor car, one walked or cycled everywhere; most of the farm workers and boys walked to work.

When I stayed with my grandmother at Somerton, one of my chief delights was to go with her on her weekly shopping expeditions to Bury. She did not keep any conveyance of her own so we were always driven in his wagonette by Mr Debenham, the landlord of the Queen Inn at Hawkedon — or 'Haardon' as we all called it less pompously.

Riding in a horse drawn vehicle was a far more enjoyable way of travelling than it is today in our speeding cars from which we can usually see so little. Then we had time to admire the landscape, comment on the crops and pass the time of day with other wayfarers and with the men working in the fields. The fact that all the menfolk who were riding in the vehicle had to get out and walk up and down any steep hill we came to, in order to help the horse, merely added spice to an enjoyable outing.

My father and one or two others were the only people in the village who, at that time, owned motor cars. The doctor did his rounds on a motorcycle and the rector, the Revd. Henry Wisdom, went everywhere on horseback. He had spent much of his life in Australia and was a familiar figure as he galloped about on his chestnut horse with his saddle bags, which were always stuffed with religious tracts, flapping behind him. The rector was not very popular, as one of his habits when visiting the cottages was to settle himself comfortably in the best armchair and, after a brief chat, spread a large handkerchief over his face and go to sleep for an hour or two. Naturally this caused some disruption to domestic life and did not greatly endear him to his flock.

Now, if I want to convince the modern sceptical young that there really was very little traffic on our country roads in those days, I tell them this little anecdote. When I was about eleven or twelve years old and rode a blue roan pony called Pax, there lived in one of the cottages just up the road from this house a Mr Gilligan, an Irishman, who went round the neighbouring villages in a flat cart drawn by a lean grey horse, from which he retailed fruit, vegetables and dried fish.

He was a merry, sportive character and whenever we chanced to meet, he in his cart, I on my pony, he would wave his whip and call out to me: 'Now, young gentleman, how about a little race?' I was all for it and without further ado away we would go, hammering along the road, neck and neck, lickety-spit, Mr Gilligan leaning forward and urging on his steed like a modern Ben Hur, while a shower of oranges, tomatoes and bloaters went sailing out over the back of his vehicle.

Although, breathless with laughter and with the effort of trying to keep up with him, I kept calling out to that determined charioteer that he was losing all his stock-in-trade overboard, he took not the least notice but merely urged on his steed to redoubled efforts. After a mile or so of this exhilarating galloping we would pull up, red in the face and thoroughly pleased with ourselves; then, chatting amiably, we would return the way we had come but at a more leisurely pace, while I helped my sporting friend to retrieve, from hedge and ditch, as much of his merchandise as we were able to locate. Were we to indulge in such antics today our expectation of life would, I imagine, be about five minutes.

None of the parish roads was tarmacadammed so far as I can recollect and generally they were quite narrow and winding, with a wide grass verge on either side between high hedges, their rough uneven surface made up of flints and granite chips, piles of which were dumped every mile or so at the road side. The village roadman, who was responsible for the upkeep of the roads, lanes and footpaths within the parish, merely tipped a shovelful of this material into any hole which developed in the surface, covered it with earth and left the passing traffic to consolidate it. A steam roller might come along later.

In summer the roads were often very dusty and birds were always to be seen taking dust baths on them or picking up grit. In August we could judge what sort of partridge season it was going to be by the number of coveys feeding and dusting on the roads. Needless to say, a combination of granite chips, flints and potholes was scarcely conducive to easy, trouble free motoring and punctures were regular and frequent.

As well as the country roads, there were a number of delightful green lanes and tracks leading to isolated farms or providing short cuts to the turnpikes. From Hartest an old pack horse track ran for some five miles from the village, past

Long's Farm and Darney's Farm, till it came out on a small side road called Golden Lane near Whepstead village. This was a perfect example of the picturesque countryside so typical of those days. Twenty feet wide, with many grassy stretches grazed smooth by cattle and horses, it was lined on both sides with trees and tall hedges and in spring and summer was a mass of wild flowers and butterflies.

Darney's Farm had been unoccupied for years; the farmhouse was in ruins, tenanted only by swallows and owls, and its orchards and meadows were overgrown and neglected. I loved going there in spring to look for orchis and to raid the magpies' nests in the thorn trees. No one else ever seemed to go there but I often saw foxes and stoats. It was a naturalist's paradise, an agro-chemist's nightmare.

There was very little public transport then between the villages and towns and many of the villagers went out of the parish only once or twice a year, usually at Christmas and Easter, to do their shopping in Bury or Sudbury. However, Walter Pawsey, the carrier, went into Bury every Wednesday, which was market day, and took passengers in his wagonette. Before leaving, he called round at the houses for a list of purchases to make in the town and in the evening he returned with his commissions completed.

While the carrier did most of our weekly shopping, my parents liked to go into Bury occasionally to shop for themselves and it was always a great event for me when I was allowed to go with them. How easy and comfortable shopping in those days was compared with the present day. Our car would make its stately progress through the streets, stopping outside any shop at which Father or Mother wished to make purchases. Out would come the shopkeeper in his white apron and complete with pencil and order pad, my parents would give their orders for groceries or fish or whatever they required and drive on.

Having completed their round of visits to the shops, they would repair to the County Club which was situated on the corner of Hatter Street and Abbeygate Street. There they drank coffee and gossiped with their friends and acquaintances, while I sat with my nose glued to the window enthralled by the people and traffic passing below. One of the sights which particularly intrigued me was that of the Marchioness of Bristol, driving herself in a small carriage drawn, if I remember right, by two or more Shetland ponies. Perched behind was a small groom in a top hat with a cockade. The Bristols of Ickworth were the most important landowners in the neighbourhood.

After an hour or two we would set off in the car — always provided that it would start — and retrace our circuit of the shops, at each of which a shop boy would appear with our purchases neatly wrapped in brown paper and tied with string, and away we would go, hopefully, for home.

Hopefully was certainly the operative word where our motoring at that period was concerned, and this would seem a suitable point at which to introduce into this narrative some of my father's cars. Father did not care for horses and we never had one except for the pony I borrowed for several of my summer holidays. Father had been trained as a naval engineer and was interested in, and adept at, all things mechanical. He was very skilful with his fingers, could draw well and in his later years spent much of his spare time making superb models of ships, particularly early ironclad warships of which he had considerable knowledge. I still have some of his models, though the majority have been lost or given away. One model of the French ironclad *'La Gloire'* is now in the Portsmouth Maritime Museum.

He was also a pioneer motorist and was one of the first people in our neighbourhood to own a motor car when, in about 1912, he bought a German Piccolo or perhaps it was an Apollo-Piccolo. It was painted bright red, had a leather clutch and was, by all accounts, singularly unreliable.

My parent appears to have terrified the entire neighbourhood with this machine which became known as 'the red peril'. His unpopularity reached its apogee on the day he encountered the Suffolk Hunt in full fig on the narrow lower road at Somerton. He was quite unable to stop Piccolo and proceeded at a spanking 20 m.p.h. straight through the entire field, scattering riders and hounds to all points of the compass. Fortunately no damage was done but it was weeks before Father dared show his face in public again.

Piccolo was somewhat before my time, though only recently I threw away an old tin of red paint which had stood for sixty years on a shelf in the coach house here, and with which Father was wont to repair the injuries to its paintwork. Mother remembered it all too well and used to describe with vivid gestures how, swathed in dust veils and a long leather motor coat, she used to make hazardous journeys round the neighbourhood at Father's side. When they came to a corner she had to cling to him to prevent herself being shot over the side into the nearest ditch. Not so fortunate was his old dog; Nep sat on the passenger seat beside him when Mother was not present, and invariably was thrown over the side as they went round a corner. Nep had to gallop behind until he could overtake and jump aboard again.

I well remember our next car, a Ford 'Tin Lizzie'. It too was pretty unreliable and seldom came home under its own power; frequently it had to be towed back from miles away by a farm horse, while Father sat grim-faced at the wheel.

After a time Mother became disenchanted with this humilitating form of locomotion and flatly refused to go out in the car, finding her bicycle more reliable. I rather enjoyed those early expeditions, but the seeds of mistrust of all mechanical vehicles were sown early, and I have always disliked and distrusted motor cars; even now, when I go out in one, I instinctively anticipate a breakdown of some sort.

Father's penultimate car was a large Wolseley, a most magnificent machine, light green in colour, with huge brass head lamps, door handles and hub caps, and a very large steering wheel. It had a canvas hood which could be folded back in fine weather and removeable celluloid side curtains through which, on a wet day, a steady spray made up of equal quantities of fresh air and rain, found its way in upon us. Goodness knows what that car's petrol consumption was but that scarcely mattered with petrol at 1s 3d (slightly over 6p) a gallon.

This imposing vehicle was far more reliable than its predecessor but Father met with a number of adventures in it. One day a motorcyclist came round a corner too fast and landed with his machine on top of my parent and his passengers when the hood was down. Another time a small child threw a stone through the windscreen; luckily Mother was sitting at the back and was not cut by the flying glass.

Later still I was riding with Father when another little incident took place. As we drove past a farm gateway a large calf, trailing a loose halter, galloped out and landed asprawl the bonnet of the car. Father, impulsive as ever, bounded out and, having hauled the calf off by its tail, proceeded to pounce on a man who was standing by the farm gate, and whom he believed was in charge of the animal, and began shaking him vigourously. I clearly remember sitting there quite entranced by the whole scene, for I had quickly realised that the unfortunate bystander had nothing whatever to do with that calf, but was Mr Polese, our village cobbler and an Italian into the bargain. All my father's natural charm, and possibly a pound note or two, were ultimately needed to smooth the cobbler's ruffled feathers.

Our family annals record one more episode in which the green Wolseley took part. Hartest's third and most picturesque pub, the Swan Inn, which was not far from our house on the Brockley road, was a beautiful old thatched building, standing well back from the road with a wide courtyard in front. The publican of that period, an old man with a beard, whom I can just remember, decided one day to cut his own throat — and proceeded to do so, though not very efficiently. As Father had one of the few cars in the village, and was nearest to the scene, he was hastily sent for to convey the old man to hospital. My mother used to recount how she accompanied them into Bury, holding a large bath towel round the injured man's neck to staunch the blood. The publican's life was saved but the whole interior of the car was awash with gore.

Sometime after that the Wolseley was sold and we acquired a more modern family saloon. The poor old Wolseley came down in the world for it was converted into a light lorry and we used to see it being driven about with a load of calves in the back. *Sic transit gloria mundi.*

3

THE OLD HOUSE

I was born in my grandmother's house in the small hamlet of Somerton and six months later came to live at Hartest Place, which has been the centre of my life for almost seventy years.

It lies on the outskirts of the village of Hartest, some two miles by road from my birthplace but less, as the pigeon flies, across the fields. My rather desultory researches over the years have failed to reveal as much about its past history as I would have liked. Some confusion has arisen because it was sometimes referred to in the past as Hartest Lodge and, furthermore, there is also in the village another old farmhouse, called Place Farm, and the two have long been closely associated.

Hartest Place once formed part of the Boxted Hall estate and is mentioned often in Poley Deeds and documents from the early 1700s. My mother bought it in the 1930s after we had occupied it as tenants for nearly twenty years. Before that her widowed great-aunt, Finetta Maddy, had lived in the house for twenty-five years.

The old house must have filled many roles during its long history. It was probably the home, for much of its existence, of yeoman or tenant farmers who cultivated the land which lay roundabout. The *Tithe Register* of 1841 lists it as having fourteen acres of land contained in a number of enclosures which were probably small meadows. Sadly, the interesting names recorded therein for fields and meadows have been lost in the mists of time.

Up to the Second World War there were four old meadows with high hedges, thick-set with oak and elm trees, in front of the house. They had once formed part of the church glebe and were farmed for nearly fifty years by the celebrated Dr John Maddy, rector of Somerton, canon of Ely and chaplain to four sovereigns, who also held at one and the same time the livings of Hartest and three other parishes, and who married as his second wife my great-great-aunt Finetta Maddy of Somerton. The house looked out upon what was always known as Maddy's Meadow until, during the last war, it was ploughed up and incorporated with three other meadows and three arable fields into one huge featureless expanse, so typical of much of the modern Suffolk countryside.

Others known to have occupied the house in the past included a doctor, a schoolmaster and a curate, the Revd William Weller-Poley. It is also said that Hartest Place was a police stattion at one time.

Suffolk is renowned for the number of its farms and manor houses; often these date back to Tudor times and display a common characteristic in their construction of lath and plaster, brick and timber. This house is a typical example. It is a listed building, displaying features of a number of periods from the fifteenth century and even earlier. Its outside walls are colour washed in traditional Suffolk pink and its roof of small brown tiles has been weathered by the passing of the years to a rich amalgam of sepia, black and red.

From outside the house looks quite large, an impression heightened by its irregular shape and the massive group of four octagonal chimneys which dominates the roof line. The effect of size is added to by the three-storeyed Georgian front with its wide sash windows, one of which is false, and its tall, pillared porch.

Like so many old houses of its kind, Hartest Place has been altered in various ways over the years, both inside and out, from its original shape and plan.

My parents altered and improved it indoors, in particular

by installing in the hall some very fine Jacobean panelling which they found on the walls of the harness room, concealed under layers of paint and whitewash. It must have come from the house at some period, possibly from our present pantry which, because of the fine carving on the ceiling beams, is thought to have been one of the main living rooms of the fifteenth century house.

Within, the house is a glorious rambling old place with its four stairways, landings and passageways, its attics and cellars and innumerable dark cupboards, the whole place ideal for small people to explore and in which to play hide-and-seek. A young cousin was once heard to say of the old house. 'It's all so exciting. In it you never know what you're going to come across next.' More recently, when the fire brigade had been called to deal with a chimney fire, a young fireman got lost in all its twists and turns and his pitiful cries of 'Where am I, I'm lost' echoed down the passages, sending us all into fits of laughter.

Besides the broad front stairs which lead up and then round to a wide landing and the two main bedrooms, the house also boasts three other stairways, one of which is a remnant of the spiral oak staircase of the old house. The attic to which it gives access has what are probably its original hand sawn oak floorboards, very rough and uneven and still bearing the toothmarks of immemorial rats. Another attic contains an example of a small and rather unusual swans egg oval fireplace. A similar fireplace was found, and then bricked up again, in the passageway leading to one of the oldest rooms in the house, with three outside walls. It was once my nursery. When, during renovations some years ago, the plaster on one of its walls was stripped away, the original old wattle and daub infilling between the studs was revealed, its ash faggots still quite recognisable though probably several centuries old.

Right up until the outbreak of the last war, when life in a rambling, inconvenient old house such as ours began to present unexpected problems — not least the lack of domestic help — we as a family spent a large part of our waking hours indoors in one or other of the reception rooms — dining room, drawing room and smoking room. They are typically Georgian, high ceilinged and airy, with tall sash windows and large open fireplaces. The drawing room faces south and has French windows at one end opening on to a verandah and the garden beyond. On that fateful September day in 1939, my mother, grandmother and I sat there in the sunshine while we listened to the voice of Neville Chamberlain announcing over the radio that Britain and Germany were at war.

Delightfully cool and airy as our living rooms are on a hot summer's day, in winter they are perishingly cold — or rather they were — until central heating was installed some years ago. The log fires over which we used to huddle did little to stave off the icy blasts which followed us about the house, even into the bathroom, but we rarely complained of the cold. Country folk in those days were a hardy breed. Only recently has a combination of double glazing and central heating brought comfort in winter to the not so young. Even so, my mother, then in her eighties, continued quite happily to sleep, as she had done since my father's death thirty years before, in one of the largest and coldest rooms in the house. He had suffered from serious heart trouble for many years, but insisted on living a normal life. He died suddenly in 1938. It was pure chance that I was at home, as the next day I was to leave for a bird watching trip to Cyprus.

Our friends and neighbours were either shocked or amused by a little tale Mother used to tell them during the arctic winter of 1962-63. She always slept badly and passed the night hours making and drinking inumerable cups of tea. One night, having taken a few sips, she put her cup down on the bedside table and dozed off: when, some time later, she roused herself and decided to finish her tea, it was frozen solid in the cup!

The one room in the house that has always been warm, snug and full of the most delicious smells is, of course, the kitchen. It is a fine room, floored with large russet and yellow tiles, its ceiling supported by many oak beams, the largest of which is a spectacular eighteen feet in length and as big round as a man's body, iron hard and blackened by the smoke of centuries. I wish I knew where the great oak tree grew from which it was cut and shaped so long ago by craftsmen using only the most primitive tools. How too was it raised up and secured in its present position where it supports most of the upper storey of the old house?

The kitchen contains a number of other striking features, particularly the Elizabethan chimney breast, much of which still survives, though its vast iron cooking stove, a relic of Victorian days, was removed some time in the 1920s. I remember it well, huge and black-leaded, with its roaring coal fire and clanking oven-doors, and I remember also what delicious odours of cakes and tarts and roast meats arose when the oven doors were opened by the reigning priestess of the kitchen.

Against the opposite wall, reaching from the floor to ceiling, is a tall old wooden dresser, much scarred by long use, on which our blue and gold family dinner service has always been displayed, topped by a number of shining dish covers. They look well against the soft Suffolk pink of the walls.

Apart from its great oak beam, the kitchen's most striking feature is its arched central window of small diamond shaped panes. I have always understood it to be a Venetian window, dating from the 1800s when a number of such windows were installed in East Anglican country houses. Our window was blown in by the explosion of a flying bomb during the war, but has been expertly restored.

At night a heavy wooden shutter is always drawn across the window. When, as a child, I slept in the room above the kitchen, I was regularly wakened by the squeal of the runners as the cook opened the shutter when she went down in the morning.

Clamped to a beam near the window are two old pepper or coffee mills. I do not remember them ever being put to their proper use, but they have always been an irresistible attraction to the young who, as soon as they set eyes upon them, must rush over and start cranking the handles amid squeals of delight. At that age I never tired of doing so myself.

What a lot of human endeavour, what joys and sorrows, what high dramas even, that old kitchen must have witnessed during its long existence as the focus and centre of life of so many rural households. I can recall happenings there which may not have been high drama but were certainly comedy.

In one corner of the kitchen is a small cupboard in which bread and groceries are stored. One evening my mother, chancing to go into the kitchen on some errand, discovered to their mutual embarrassment, our village copper, a rather large man who was courting one of our domestics at that time. On hearing Mother's approach, he attempted the impossible — to hide himself in the cupboard among the jam pots and bread bins. It ended with much hilarity all round, and thereafter the cupboard has always been known as the policemans cupboard.

I have vivid recollections of an oft-repeated scene that used to take place at one period of my childhood, around the kitchen table. My parents had given me a pogo stick, a toy all the rage then among the young. It consisted of a stout pole with a metal crossbar attached to a very strong spring. By holding the pole with both hands, putting both feet on on the crossbar and alternatively depressing and releasing the spring by adjusting one's weight, it was possible for an expert operator to progress about in huge and exhilarating leaps. Unfortunately, I was not heavy enough to make the pogo stick work properly, but our cook of that period, a sturdy maiden named Ena, soon mastered the art and delighted onlookers by bounding about her kitchen on my toy.

News of her performances soon spread to the front of the house and Father demanded a demonstration. He was so taken with the sight — he loved anything amusing and unusual — that, until the novelty wore off, he insisted on taking friends who happened to call upon us into the kitchen where he persuaded Ena to demonstrate her skill on the pogo stick.

The tale of our cook springing round the kitchen like a large kangaroo in a blue apron, greatly tickled the neighbourhood and soon spread far and wide, bringing fame to our old kitchen.

Down a brick floored passage beyond the kitchen lie its essential offices; a store cupboard which always smells of parrafin, polish and mice, a pantry, larder and scullery.

Our larder was once the old dairy, with slatted walls and a paved floor for coolness. It is always full of produce, most of it home-grown. Its shelves are loaded with bottled fruit, jams and pickles, while the floor is occupied by earthenware crocks of eggs preserved in isinglass, and beans in salt. We have no fridge or deep freeze, our dark, cool cellars having long proved sufficient for our needs. Once a year, right up to the outbreak of the last war, the shelves of the larder would be piled with hams, brawns and sausages, following the slaughter of one of our own pigs.

Our scullery must always, I suppose have been the most important part of the domestic back premises of the old house. It is a long sunny room looking out over the stable yard and over the years would have been an excellent place from which the domestics of the day could, and no doubt did, exchange ribaldry with the grooms and gardeners employed about the place. Within, one wall is largely occupied by wooden dressers and cupboards, plate racks and stone sinks supplied with water from storage tanks at the top of the house. There was also, throughout my childhood, a hand pump which supplied the sinks with soft water from a well outside in the yard, its loud clanking sounding intermittently throughout the day. My young friends and I greatly enjoyed working the handle up and down to bring the water gushing out from the mouth of the pump — something far more interesting then merely turning on a tap.

The opposite wall of the scullery is occupied by relics of the past — an arched brick baking oven and a copper in which our predecessors brewed their own beer. Neither, so far as I recall, have been used during my lifetime, but a large soft-water copper, heated by a coal fire, is in constant use for the important task of washing the brick floors of kitchen and passages.

In my young days the most interesting feature of the scullery was always the wide, open fireplace, large enough for a grown man to stand in, and into which I loved to scramble to look up into the great sooty tunnel of the chimney. Far above I could see the blue sky with its wheeling swallows, some of which built their mud nests around the inside of the chimney. That fireplace seems to have been designed solely for the purpose of smoking hams. The grate is wide enough to hold an entire faggot and all round the inside of the chimney, for some ten feet up, are still to be seen the old iron bars from which many generations of Suffolk housewives hung their home cured hams.

Friends and acquaintances who visit the house for the first time often exclaim in surprise at the number and extent of our outbuildings. We explain that, besides being a private house, Hartest Place has also been the home of working farmers who needed stables, barns, store sheds and outhouses to accommodate their livestock and farm implements.

The back of the house overlooks the stable yard which was once cobbled but is now grassed over and kept under control by the industrious grazing of a flock of white rabbits, highly decorative and excellent for training gun dog puppies to be steady to fur. The main block of our outbuildings, which should, I suppose, be called the barn, though we have never referred to it as such, takes up almost the whole of one side of the yard. It is of typical timber and plaster construction with a slate roof, though it would certainly have been thatched originally.

The old coach house, now our garage, occupies the middle of the block and on either side are stables with stalls and a loose box, as well as what is commonly called a nag stable where we have always kept our pigs. There is also a large wood shed and the old harness room. The hay loft above, with its lofty timbered roof, runs the whole length of the building with openings in the floor through which the hay was thrown down to the stables below. Large wooden bins for corn and chaff occupy one end. Outside the stables is an old stone mounting block used in the past by riders of both sexes, and particularly ladies in riding habits, for ease and convenience in getting on and off their horses.

Until fairly recently there were, at the back of the barn, two very dilapidated ivy covered sheds in which farm implements and stock were once housed. When they were no longer usable for any purpose I had them demolished, leaving only flint and brick walls. On the gable end of one, under its protective screen of ivy, we found, inscribed in the old plaster, the date 1553.

All the walls surrounding the yard are of flint and brick, so typical of our part of Suffolk, were the soil seems to grow flints as prolifically as it grows sugar beet. On one wall a large house leek has taken root. I have admired it ever since I first set eyes upon it as a very small child. Growing steadily year by year, it is now quite enormous and must be at least one hundred years old.

On the opposite side of the yard, built against the curve of the garden wall, is a range of small outhouses. At the end nearest to the house are two of what were once very necessary accessories to rural life before the advent of piped water. They are earth privies, each a two-seater as was formerly the custom in village homes. I have even seen a three-seater with a small hole provided for children.

How well I remember a minor tragi-comedy connected with one of those outdoor earth privies. We had been given a cat, a wild little thing that lived in the stables. One day it took fright at something and was seen by our garden boy to dash through the open door of the domestics loo and disappear down one of the dark holes in the seat. Naturally this caused distress and concern; people peered down into the horrid depths calling 'puss puss' but all to no avail. After a time it was assumed that the cat had met a terrible death in the dark abyss.

However, all ended happily when, some days later, as the cook sat enthroned on the loo, she heard faint miaows rising from the depths. Floorboards were hastily pulled up and there sat the cat, perched on a small wooden projection above the quagmire.

I still find that jolly little tale quite a winner at lunch or dinner parties when, during a pause in the conversation, I am able to throw into the gap the remark: 'Did you ever hear how our cat went down the loo?' Cries of horror and disbelief naturally follow this statement, as most people today are unacquainted with earth privies, until I am able to explain the true circumstances.

4

VILLAGE DAYS

The village of Hartest, in which I have spent some of the happiest years of my life, is one of the most picturesque of our small Suffolk villages, though it is comparatively little known, except by artists, as it lies somewhat off the beaten track. It nestles in a valley through which flows a small stream, a tributary of the River Glem, but nameless on all the maps I have ever seen, though known to us in the village as the Smithbrook. There are a number of other Smithbrooks and Smithwoods in Suffolk.

In appearance our village has not altered very much during my lifetime. Sadly, a number of its old thatched cottages have been demolished to make room for more modern homes, but otherwise most of the new building has been confined to its outskirts. The heart of the village is still its wide Green, round the margin of which stood, until some thirty years ago, an irregular screen of venerable elm and ash trees. When, with the passage of time, the old trees became dangerous and had to be cut down; they were replaced at the time of our Queen's coronation with an avenue of lime trees and sycamores and a number of pink mays and horse chestnuts grouped just outside the church wall. A few of the more elderly trees have so far survived.

Much of the charm of Hartest Green lies in the fact that no two of the houses that enfold it are alike; they are all old and each has its own design and character. Some are thatched, more are of colour washed plaster roofed with small red Suffolk tiles, a few glow with the mellow red of Georgian brick. The whole effect is an irregular facade of design and colour delightful to the eye.

As I recall it from my childhood The Green was a more picturesque and bustling place that it is today. There were more shops then, and more noise and movement on The Green itself where chickens and ducks wandered at will and a flock of geese shared the grazing with Ellinghams' cream-coloured ponies.

Other prominent features of the village scene then were the two hand pumps, round one or other of which there seemed always to be someone with a bucket — for piped water did not reach the village until the 1950s; the wood yard where timber for wagons and wagon wheels was seasoned; the blacksmith's forge sheltering under its old elms and the famous Hartest Stone.

Of all those once familiar landmarks the Hartest Stone alone has survived the passage of time. This huge, flat-topped granite boulder of glacial origin was found on what was known in former days as Somerton Common — though in my youth it was always called 'The Downs'. The War of the Spanish Succession, which had raged for many years, impoverishing most of the nations of Europe including Britain, came to an end in 1713 with the Treaty of Utrecht, and the people of Hartest and Somerton decided to commemmorate the occasion by moving the great stone down to Hartest Green.

A wooden sledge was constructed for its transport and forty horses were loaned by neighbouring farmers to pull it, with a trumpeter playing merry tunes mounted aloft, down to Hartest where it was deposited on The Green. There it has stood ever since, its surface polished smooth by the sit-upons of generations of Hartest children, mine among them.

My uncle, Arthur Gray, who was brought up here at Hartest Place, always asserted that it was originally intended to take The Stone on to Bury St Edmunds but that it never got farther than Hartest because the sledge broke up here under the weight.

Among the many trees that once stood around the margins of The Green and beneath which generations of Hartest folk have sheltered from sun and tempest, I particularly recall two groups of old pollard elms, short, squat and often hollow, with branches sweeping almost to the ground; one group stood close by the blacksmith's forge, the other by the chapel. When the passing years took their toll and the old trees fell or had to be cut down, for some of them were mere hollow shells, they were greatly mourned by the children of the village, for all of us had spent many happy hours building tree houses in them or clambering and swinging about like small Tarzans in their branches.

In those long past days we country children had comparatively few of the amusements and entertainments now taken for granted by the modern young. We simply devised our own. Most of them had to take place outdoors, for there was little room in the cottages for childish games. The wireless was still in its crystal and cat's whisker stage and very few houses in our village had a set. We hadn't one, nor did I wish for one when there were so many more interesting things to be done outdoors in the farmyards, fields and woods. When it was fine we played on the straw stacks or dammed up the brook to provide pools in which we could float home made toy boats, or paddle and bathe in hot weather. When it was wet, we amused ourselves in the big barns, clambering up into the cobwebby beams or playing hide-and-seek in the hay lofts and granaries, where sometimes we had the added excitement of being found and chased out by an irate farmer.

In the spring most boys and some girls went birds' nesting, the chief sufferers being blackbirds and thrushes which were then so common everywhere. Usually their eggs were eaten, after being hard boiled in a tin over a fire of sticks, but sometimes, sadly, they were merely used as marbles or thrown against tree trunks out of sheer devilment. A few of us collected birds' eggs seriously, blowing them with a hole pricked at each

49

end with a thorn or a pin, but few boys kept up their egg collecting once they became interested in girls.

One of the springtime events to which all Hartest children looked forward was the annual visit of the fair which used to spend three days each April on our Green. I was fascinated by it all; the brightly painted caravans with their gleaming brass water cans and attendant horses and dogs, the side shows and swing boats and especially the roundabouts with their gaily hued horses and cockerels on which I went round and round as long as my pennies lasted, amid their lively honky-tonk music. As we were a very unmusical family I particularly enjoyed the novelty of bands and the cheerful fairground music.

The fair was run by the Wright family from Lawshall and Mrs Wright, the matriach, presided over the whole operation. I remember her well, sitting on the steps of her caravan in a huge hat decorated with black ostrich feathers, while she kept a strict eye on all that went on and handed out tickets for free rides on the roundabouts to any child who looked hard-up and deserving.

When summer came round — and all Suffolk summers seem, in retrospect, to have been endlessly sunny — there were still more activities to keep us happy; fishing and swimming, more birds' nesting, helping on the farms at haytime — we called it haysel, a word not, I think, to be found in dictionaires — and in the harvest fields when we were allowed to ride on or lead the horses which hauled the great creaking wagons.

Sometimes, when a summer's day promised to be particularly fine, Father and Mother would take me and one or two friends for a boating outing on the River Stour at Sudbury, or even as far as Brandon, where we hired a boat from The Ouse Hotel alongside the old Roman bridge over the river.

That was one of my greatest treats, for to get there meant crossing the wild wasteland of the Breck with its vast expanse of heather, sand and furze which stretched away to the horizon on all sides. This was before the planting of the great gloomy forest which now covers the Breck.

My father was a good oarsman and he had taught me to row properly. We used to paddle upstream looking down at the shoals of dace and other fish dashing past below, and admiring the blue and black dragonflies which hovered about the waterside herbage. Best of all we could usually rely on seeing, while we ate our picnic lunch on the bank, a family party of Montagu's harriers — now so rare in Britain — sailing about over the water meadows. The day always ended with an enormous tea on the hotel lawn overlooking the river.

Winter brought different but equally enjoyable diversions. When frost and snow gripped the land there was sliding or skating on the local ponds, or on the moat at Boxted, and tobogganing on the snowy slopes above the village.

I do not recollect that Hartest boys were then much interested in football, though by the 1930s friendly games against neighbouring villages were often played on Maddy's Meadow, which lay just beyond the garden here.

For me, colour and excitement was always added to the scene when the hounds met on Hartest Green, and I could follow them on my cycle. In the course of time, I learned all the best places in which to position myself to see the hounds running and, if I were lucky, to view the fox. Later I went over to Thurlow sometimes to follow the hounds there and to stay overnight with my friend Lance le Fleming, who loved fox hunting, and acted for some years as terrier man for the Newmarket and Thurlow Hunt. I still have, hanging on my sitting room wall, a fox's brush given me by the Master after I had been in at a kill.

In those days we saw much more of the hunt than we do now. For one thing hounds always travelled from their kennels to the meet on foot; they were not boxed to and fro as is the case nowadays, so frequently we met the whole pack jogging along the road, the pink coats of Huntsman and Whips adding a welcome splash of colour to a dull winter's day.

Besides those simple country amusements which I shared with my young friends in the village, I also took part —

51

sometimes rather reluctantly — in most of the activities then available to the children of reasonably well-to-do country families. In summer there was an almost continous stream of tennis and croquet parties and other outdoor games, all of which ended with gargantuan teas. Most of us had bicycles on which we pedalled busily about; a few lucky ones had ponies.

Looking back now to those distant days and events, I cannot remember that I was ever bored. If we found ourselves at a loose end, my companions and I could always fall back on age-old childish diversion, such as seeing who could climb highest in a tree, dabbling bare-foot in the brook or stealing rides on the farm horses; in autumn we all played conkers, at least half of the fun of which consisted in searching for a possible champion among the shiny brown nuts as they came showering down from the chestnut trees.

I have always been interested in and intrigued by the old village place names, and by the names of the farms, the woods and the individual fields that make up (or used to make up) our village lanscape. From them we can often learn a little about the past history of an old building or group of cottages, or even about the past use of some particular field such as Maddy's Meadow to which I have already referred.

Until the agricultural slaughter of the hedges and field boundaries that took place in East Anglia just after the last war — and which still goes on — almost all fields and meadows on almost all farms had individual names describing their particular shape, or size or soil qualities; names like High Hilly, Brecky Ley, The Seven Acres, Church Field or Plumtree Meadow had been known and used almost daily by generations of farmers and farmworkers since the time of the Enclosures Acts that first brought the fields into being.

The origin of some names are obvious, at others we can make a fair guess, but all too often the name goes back so far into the past that even the most intensive research into property deals or church and parish records will tell us nothing.

How nice if we could know more. Why for instance is Blue Hog Lane in this village so named? Whose was the blue hog, and when and why did it give its name to what is a small and comparatively unremarkable little lane leading down to Long's Farm from the Brockley Road?

Why are Potash and Tan Office Farm, The Hatch and The Duddery so called? Archivists believe that the first two names commemmorate past village industries; it is certainly a fact that a certain John Frost, a tanner, lived somewhere near where Tan Office Farm now stands, in the seventeenth century. I remember The Hatch when it was just a group of derelict cottages, haunted by swallows and bats. As for The Duddery, it was the name given to a row of old half-timbered cottages between the church and the river. I can just remember them. They were pulled down long ago, but the name has survived. As Hartest was at one time the home of weavers employed in the wool and cloth trade, it seems likely that the ancient name derives from the period when people who made cheap clothes, or 'duds', lived in the cottages.

In my youth I was often told a nice little anecdote connected with The Duddery. One night, long years ago, an old couple who were asleep upstairs in one of the cottages there, heard strange noises coming from below. Investigation revealed a large elephant busy helping itself to any food it could lay its trunk on in the kitchen. It had escaped from a travelling circus which was giving shows on Hartest Green and had somehow found its way in through the front door. Unfortunately it was unable, or unwilling, to leave by the same route and in the end, so the story goes, the front door and part of the wall had to be removed before Jumbo was persuaded to depart — backwards?

The names of some of our local farms — Cook's, Long's, Spencer's and Townsend's — commemmorate previous owners or tenants, while the origin of names like Pear Tree Farm and Hill Farm are obvious. Probably only our older inhabitants will know why Swan Farm is so called; the fields and buildings belonging to it at one time encompassed the Swan Inn, a very old and picturesqeue thatched building standing back in its courtyard off the Brockley road, and which was burned to the ground sometime in the 1920s.

Our Burnt House Farm has the distinction of having earned its name at least twice. I can just recall the second occasion when it caught fire. I was about five or six years old and it was also the last time that I saw Hartest's old fire engine in action. This ancient little machine was hand operated. It was painted bright red and, unless my memory is faulty, it had a small brass chimney. It was kept in a barn at Hop Hall — and what, incidentally, can be the origin of that name? Was its garden noted for wild hops?

When the call came for the engine some convenient horse had to be taken out of its stable or pasture and harnessed to the machine. Then off it went at a stately gallop, picking up the volunteer firemen on the way. At the fire the hose was run out to the nearest pond or brook and, with the firemen and anyone else who cared to join in, busily working the handles on either side of the machine, a rather feeble jet of water was produced. Because of the inevitable delay in catching and harnessing the horse, and then in getting the machine and the firemen to the scene of operations, the house or barn on fire had generally burned down before the machine really got going. I wonder what happened to that old engine; it was a real museum piece even in those days.

On the subject of village fire engines, I well remember the hostler at the Perseverance Inn by Long Melford Railway station amusing my father and me with an account of the old Melford fire brigade, of which I think he had been a member.

Their machine was probably about the same vintage as the Hartest engine, though obviously much bigger. It was drawn by the old horse that normally pulled the refuse cart. The firemen were all part-timers and getting old too; some could scarcely clamber on to the machine. To keep up their strength they always carried a crock of beer with them and on arrival at the scene of the fire enquired if the building were insured to make certain of getting their pay.

Once, when the engine was making its stately way to a fire,

with the beer crock already circulating, an artist was observed
sketching by the roadside and the driver of the fire engine was
told to slow down in hope that the artist would have time to
put it, and its crew, into his picture.

5

VILLAGE CHARACTERS

In my young days, interesting and colourful characters, some of them delightfully eccentric, were far more common in our Suffolk villages than they are today, when political and educational trends are doing their best to squeeze everyone into a dull uniform mould.

We had our share in Hartest, and I particularly recall our village postmen who played such an important part in our daily lives when the telephone was still a rarity in rural homes. Prominent among them was Mr Ling, who drove the mail cart. To my childish eyes he appeared to be an indubitable pirate, for he had a wooden leg and often wore a red stocking-cap hanging down over one eye.

I was much in awe of him, but finally he became a close friend after I had innocently posted a very precious toy dog called Tray in our private letter box at the bottom of the drive. Most country houses in those days had their own post boxes for which a small rent was paid to the GPO. I thought Tray had gone for ever, but a day or two later Ling stumped up to the back door where he insisted on delivering the missing Tray back into my arms personally. The toy had, apparently, caused considerable puzzlement at the Bury sorting office, and then amusement when Ling, luckily remembered where he had picked it up.

His was the last of the horse drawn mail carts, its place being taken a few years later by the cycling postman John Sturgeon, friendly and helpful to all and a passionate musician. Every weekday morning, wet or fine, sun or hail, he cycled the nine miles into Bury, carrying the village mail in a bag on his back and returned again in the afternoon, bringing letters and parcels, including *The Times* for Father, which he delivered round the village before his day's work was done. He used to relate how he had bought his cottage for £6 as it stood and then had to remove it piecemeal, bricks, timber and all, from its old site, where the new village hall was about to be built, and re-erect it elsewhere in the village. It is still there.

Arnie Cadge was another postman character. Nearly as broad as he was tall, he had for years done the Somerton postal round, there being no post office in that small hamlet. Travelling by footpaths and short cuts, he carried the mail, heavy parcels included, often through deep snow and the Suffolk winter's mud, delivering the odd letter or parcel to many an outlying farm and cottage. His round ended each day about mid-afternoon when he would come trudging up the lane past our house, often tired but always ready to stop and relay gossip.

Another Sturgeon was the village piano tuner and clock winder. He was a familiar sight as he went on his daily rounds on foot, a tall old man with a white beard, in an old fashioned frock coat and billy cock hat. He would visit all the big houses to wind their clocks and to do necessary repairs, as well as tuning their pianos.

Many of the farm labourers and craftsmen in the village were also characters in their own right, skilful in their work, original in garb and conversation. Two old men who worked at Pickles Farm, and went past our house every day, were alike as two peas, bearded, wearing bowler hats green with age, the thickest of flannel shirts, even in high summer, and corduroy trousers fastened below the knee with leather straps. One of them, whom Father had unkindly nicknamed the 'Grandfather of all Rabbits', is associated in my mind with a little episode when I was probably about four or five years old. It was very cold, with deep snow on the ground, and my nanny had taken me down to the village on some errand. Presently, lurching and staggering towards us through the snow, came 'Grandfather of all Rabbits'.

'Look at that poor man, is he ill?' I am supposed to have asked my nanny, but she, who had quickly realised that he was merely much the worse for drink, hastily swept me off home. He was the first drunken man I had ever seen.

I have already mentioned our rector, the Revd Henry Wisdom, a famous character who galloped about the parish on his great horse, scattering low church pamphlets wherever he went, and often going off to sleep with a handkerchief over his face in the cottages he had ostensibly gone to visit.

A near neighbour of ours and another true Suffolk character was Tom Cornish, the thatcher. Highly skilled in his trade, he was in constant demand to thatch houses and stacks in the neighbourhood. He had never been to school, could not read nor write and was, I suppose, a real primitive by modern standards. It was said that Tom never threw away a waist coat but when one became worn out he simply added another one on top of it. He always brewed his own beer and to do so used to borrow our water-cart, which he filled up from the horse pond down the lane, despite the fact that the water was thick as pea soup and had been used by the farm animals for purposes other than drinking. Tom said that it made 'wonnerful good beer'. He spoke the broadest Suffolk, so much so that strangers often had difficulty in understanding much of what he had to say and Father always tried, when we had visitors staying with us, to get Tom to come and have a conversation with them. He might have come from Borneo or the Philippine Islands for all their understanding of his conversation. His family caught all their drinking water in a bucket, placed at the mouth of a field drain outside his cottage. So too did William Hunt, our gamekeeper, away in the fields at Somerton. But both lived to a considerable age.

Almost up to the outbreak of the last war, the old Suffolk dialect, with its local variants, was widely spoken in the villages by old and young alike. This included all stratas of society — the gentry, doctors and parsons, vets and farmers — unless, of course, they were "foreigners", the word we applied to all those who had not lived in the villages for at least twenty years. Our local baronet always spoke broad Suffolk to his farm men and beaters or when he was out hunting, and my parents and I regularly used Suffolk words and expressions when talking among ourselves.

It was quite normal practice, but one of our visitors was said to have been astonished and midly shocked when she was out for a walk with me and I greeted a countryman of my acquaintance with the traditional Suffolk greeting 'worcher bor' which meant roughly, 'Hello, how are you?' The word bor, usually pronounced bu as in but, is presumably a corruption of boy, though it was applied to males of all ages, females were merely gals or real little mawthers. Nowadays, though a few of us old uns still use dialect words and expressions, the modern young in the villages converse in a horrible mixture of basic and posh words, including Americanisms which they learnt at school or pick up from the radio and television. Sadly, the use of Suffolk vernacular words is fast dying out.

One well-known character who passed our house regularly every weekend for many years was a farmer and corn merchant who lived near Sudbury, but also farmed land at Brockley, the next parish to Hartest. Every Saturday morning he walked the ten miles from his home in order to visit his Brockley farm.

He was a formidable looking old gentleman as he strode by, spectacles gleaming, watch chain a-swing and large walking stick thumping the road. It was difficult to get even a good morning out of him. On Sunday he would make his way back home in the same manner. He did not possess a car and the uncharitable said that he walked the ten miles each way at a weekend in order to save the bus fare. Needless to say, he died a rich man.

Another regular visitor to our village during my childhood was an itinerant rag and bone man. I never knew his name but nonetheless had a keen financial interest in his visits. On the day when I expected him to come rattling past in his pony and trap I would be anxiously awaiting his arrival at our gate.

I could hear him coming all the way from Brockley, for he advertised his progress by a loud refrain which he repeated every few minutes as he jogged along. It went — and I can hear it now though it must be all of seventy years since I last heard the sound ringing across our quiet Suffolk fields: 'Rags-y-bones, rags-y-bones-y-rabbit skins — any old lumbaar.'

Seeing me waiting at the gate, he would pull up with a polite dab at his cap and ask what I had for him that day. What I had varied from week to week and depended on my success with trap and gun.

If things had gone well I had probably three or four mole skins which would have been pegged out flat in the sun to dry and possibly one or two rabbit skins. For the mole skins I hoped for four pennies each and for the rabbits tuppence a piece. The proceeds went straight into my piggy bank of the period, to join the three pennies I received each week as pocket money.

Hartest also boasted someone who, in former times, would have been looked upon as a witch. She was an old woman who lived by herself in a thatched cottage which has since been pulled down. She was known as Black Sal, kept a large number of cats and smoked a pipe. No-one ever dared to venture into her dark and smoky cottage but the boys of the village enjoyed tormenting her in a mild way. I have no idea how she lived or what money she had but she appeared always to have something cooking, and possibly her neighbours helped her out. She was a weird looking old scarecrow and in appearance certainly lived up to her name.

When she finally fell ill and had to be taken away to hospital, where the poor old thing died, the village nurse reported to my mother that she had found Black Sal inside an old feather mattress with only her head sticking out, and it had been necessary to pluck her to remove the feathers, adhering to her body before she was fit to be removed to hospital.

At Somerton there also lived another quaint old woman who would almost have qualified for the title of witch. Her name was Miss Maidwell and, in theory, she kept a small shop, but no-one, so far as I am aware, ever bought anything from her and indeed her stock in trade consisted of no more than a few dirty faded books propped up in the window of her cottage. Unlike Black Sal, who never seemed to budge from her cottage, Miss Maidwell was always out and about, collecting sticks for her fire and blackberries and other fruit for her meals.

It was said that on one occasion she ventured to travel by the carrier's cart into Bury to do some shopping, but having missed the transport home, she decided to start walking back to Somerton. Soon, getting tired, she went to sleep in a ditch and was found there next morning, having sustained herself overnight with a meal of raw bloaters. For some obscure reason she carried on a fierce vendetta against my uncle, the rector, and once attacked him with a pitchfork.

It is interesting that in the past Hartest is said to have had a real witch, or at least one who was accused of being such. In 1694 Widow Munnings of Hartest appeared at Bury Assizes under four charges of witchcraft. Rather remarkably for those times, she was acquitted of them all and died peacefully two years later in the village.

I have left to the end the most outstanding local character of my childhood; this was a near neighbour, John George Weller-Poley of Boxted Hall, known far and wide as Squire Poley. Owning the entire parish of Boxted and land in most of its adjoining parishes including Hartest, he was one of the last of the rural squires. He and his delightful wife were very close friends of ours and scarcely a week went by throughout the year in which we did not see something of them, or in which we were not invited there to have tea or to play bridge or croquet, to fish, punt on the moat or to shoot.

When I first remember him Squire Poley was already an old man, but a very handsome and imposing one. His main recreations then consisted in summer of raking the weeds out of his moat into a punt, and of sawing logs in the stable yard in winter. He usually wore old clothes and an old hat, and at times was mistaken for his own gardener and occasionally tipped, much to his delight, by visitors who had come to call on his wife and were not already acquainted with him.

In his younger days he spent much of his time shooting and

Father, who shot with him at Boxted and Chadacre for forty years or more, had some delightful recollections to tell of Squire's shooting eccentricities. Apparently he never took more than one hundred cartridges for the day's sport and when he had fired them all, instead of borrowing more from his neighbour, as most of us would have done, he simply stopped shooting and lay on his back in the mud even though the birds were still flying over him. Also, if he were shooting as a guest on land which adjoined his estate, any pheasants which came over him and which he thought were heading towards Boxted, were allowed to pass unharmed, the squire merely waving them on with his hat. After a shoot, unless he was far from home, he always chose to walk back across country, having sent his carriage away in the morning.

A little episode which illustrates Squire Poley's sense of humour comes to mind. An old friend of Father's, Axel Franke, was staying with us and we had all been asked to tea at Boxted, where there was a large house party. Uncle Axel, as I called him, rashly volunteered to take one of the guests on the moat in a canoe and very soon upset it. Dripping with mud and weed they were taken into the house and fitted out with some of Squire Poley's clothes, being told to come back next day to retreive their own garments. When they did so, they found that all their clothes, neatly cleaned and dried, had been hung out on the iron archway at the entrance to the house.

Boxted Hall was, in those days, a veritable museum, a treasure house stuffed with the old, the beautiful and the extraodinary, an accumulation of sundries which could not fail to fascinate the young and the not so young. It was often said that nothing had been altered, nothing changed and nothing discarded in the old house for one hundred years or more.

In the panelled hall with its great fireplace, in which a log fire seemed always to be burning, the walls were covered with a glorious conglomeration of Poley and Stuart portraits, swords, cross bows and helmets, paintings of ships and battles, tapestries and stags' heads from one of which hung the gong which summoned the family to meals. I remember too the bottled ships, the tall vases full of pampas gress and peacock feathers, the cases of geological specimens, the stuffed crocodile hanging from the ceiling and — the prize attraction in my eyes — the grinning head under a glass shade, said to be that of a Maori warrior.[1]

For me, however, the sunny billiard room, overlooking the moat, held greater charms, for it was lined from end to end with cases of stuffed birds, many of them unknown to me, while on tables along one side were ranged a splendid series of life like models depicting stages of the bull fight in all its gory detail.

In a cage by the window lived a grey parrot, an ancient and extremely bad tempered bird, Mother, who had a remarkable affinity with all birds and beasts, was the only person I ever saw who could stroke Polly without being savagely bitten. I must confess that, in summer, the billiard room had for me a more mundane attraction, as a large tray of hothouse peaches was always ripening there in a sunny window. The Squire seldom let us go home without first picking out for us a box of the ripest and most luscious fruit.

One other part of Boxted Hall which was particularly enjoyed by visiting children was the long attic — known to the family as Long Melford — which ran almost the whole length of the house. There, on wet days, we were taken by our kind hostess to rummage in endless chests and cupboards full of old toys and decorations and superb old uniforms.

Squire Poley had, in springtime, another favourite diversion — the search for moorhens' eggs. Hard boiled moorhens eggs were then looked upon as great delicacies, second only to plovers' eggs, and they were collected and eaten on all the great estates as well as by most farm boys. Squire was a familiar figure as he stumped about his estate, carrying a long bamboo

---

[1] Some time ago I was interested to read in the papers that the Maori's head from Boxted Hall was being offered for sale by auction. A Maori association in New Zealand got wind of the sale and objected to it. After some negotiation Mrs Weller Poley, the owner, agreed to return the head to the land of its ancestors. She was promised some New Zealand artefact in return, but nothing ever materialised.

pole with a spoon tied to its end, visiting every pond looking for eggs. I also harvested all the moorhens eggs I could find and, as each pair has two or three broods a year, their numbers never seemed to suffer, a hard winter reducing them far more severely than egg culling.

When, as occasionally happened, we sat in the Poley family pew in Boxted church, which was away to one side of the chancel, it used to amuse us to notice that Squire Poley kept a copy or two of *'Blackwood's Magazine'* there to help him through a tedious sermon. He was a wonderful old character and a very dear friend.

6

MY ANIMAL FRIENDS

I had originally intended that this chapter should be entitled *'Family Pets'* but as so many of the birds and beasts that figure in it, and that have shared my hearth and home at various periods of my life, came to be looked upon more as family friends than as mere pets, I hope that the present title is more appropriate.

Most country children of my generation loved keeping pets and I was no exception. Apart from the usual run of the mill creatures such as tortoises, bantams, white mice — some of which escaped and founded a line of piebald house mice here — and domestic rabbits of which I acquired a great number, I was always on the look out during my forays into the fields and woods for any young wild creature that seemed likely to make an interesting pet. They were so appealing in their defencelessness and beauty and the problem of getting them to feed, and then rearing them successfully, presented me with a real challenge. As a naturalist I was able to learn more from them of their habits and way of life than I could by watching them in the wild. My poor parents never knew when I was going to appear with some wild refugee clutched firmly to my chest.

Fortunately, Mother shared my interest and coped nobly with any bird or beast I had to leave in her charge while I was away at school. Father was less enthusiastic but he put up with the miniature zoo which I amassed in my den in one of the attics.

I can still remember most of the birds and beasts that shared their brief lives with me, and the pleasure that attending to their needs and watching their daily activities gave me, until bitter experience made me realise that wild things that have lost their fear of man are liable to come to some sad and often violent end. So gradually I gave up trying to keep any wild orphan unless it could quickly be restored to its natural surroundings; otherwise too much heartbreak was involved.

Among the pets that I particularly recall were two young tawny owls I found at school and was subsequently allowed to carry to and fro between school and home. From them I learned that owls are great bathers, which is why so many are found drowned in water troughs used by cattle and horses. I also acquired, straight from the nest, several jackdaws and jays. These amusing, clever, mischievous creatures stole small shiny objects from our rooms, and one used to bomb us with pats of butter which it filched from the table when we lunched outdoors.

There were also a number of hedgehogs which were very easily tamed and which came regularly to eat bread and milk from a saucer on the lawn. I had a cuckoo — a most voracious creature with its ever open orange mouth — doves and pigeons, and a number of small wild rabbits. One of the latter was so tame that I could carry him about everywhere in my pocket. I used to take him with me to the village sweet shop, kept by Miss Pask, a particular pal of mine. There he was allowed to sit on the counter and nibble biscuits.

I was never lucky enough to acquire a young squirrel or a badger, which I would dearly have liked, and Father firmly banned any fox cub that I was offered. However, I got to know one of the latter, which a friend and neighbour brought down from Scotland. When his owner was away from home I used to take the little fox, whose name was Fergus, for walks and soon I became much attached to the delightful creature. His speed and agility in weaving his way through thick undergrowth, or when jumping over or through some obstacle, were wonderful to see. Those who hunt or shoot see many instances of this lightening agility when a fox breaks cover, sees danger ahead and dives back into shelter in a flash. Fergus amused and charmed me with his habits. He loved fruit and would delicately nip blackberries and gooseberries off the bushes without pricking his nose on the thorns. Poor little fox, his natural instinct as a chicken killer led to his undoing.

One of my more unusual pets was a long-eared owl that I found as a nestling in a wood in Northern Ireland. It was about the size, shape and colour of a fluffy tennis ball, with orange eyes and two diminutive lumps on top of its head, which were its incipient ear tufts. It travelled back to Suffolk with me. The sea crossing was very rough and I am a very bad sailor; so apparently was the owl, for as I lay in my bunk, feeling near to death, I could see the little bird clinging to the edge of the wash-basin and giving every indication that it too was suffering from *mal de mer*.

When we boarded the train, I had to put the owl, which subsequently became known as 'Peppery', in its cardboard travelling box on the rack. In the carriage with me were a number of elderly gentlemen, all busy reading their newspapers. Soon their concentration was disturbed by sounds of pecking and hiccuping from Peppery's box above my head. I could scarely contain my amusement at the expressions on their faces as each gentleman looked enquiringly at his neighbour to see if he were responsible for the strange noises. Then, one more alert than the rest, located the source of the squeaks and rattles and demanded that I reveal what was in the box. So the little bird was taken out and travelled for the rest of the journey to London, sitting on my knee, much admired by my fellow passengers.

Peppery grew into a very beautiful bird. His black and grey pencilled plumage, deep orange eyes which seemed to glow like fire, and long ear tufts which popped up erect whenever anything interested or alarmed him, delighted all who saw him. His nights were spent in one of the stables where he could fly about and amuse himself, but during the day I took him indoors to my workroom where he sat half asleep on top of a bookcase. Any sound though, such as a fly buzzing on the widow or the rustle of a piece of paper, brought him flying down to investigate.

Sometimes while I wrote, Peppery would alight on the table and take a pen or pencil in his foot, turning it round and round and crooning to himself. He also seemed to enjoy sitting on my shoulder and gently nibbling my ears.

He was very fond of the dogs and shared the fireside with them, spreading out his wings to get the fullest benefit from the heat. He was affectionate with us all and though free winged, I could carry him about everywhere on my fist. Inevitably, he came to a sad end, when one very stormy day — it was the day on which King George V died — as I carried him across the yard to his stable on my fist, a gust of wind dislodged him and carried the poor little bird away up into the sky and out of sight. I searched for him for days and mourned his loss exceedingly.

Another unusual pet was a brown hare. I rescued him from a stoat when he was no more than a day old, a delightful soft brown creature with large golden eyes, long whiskers and a white star on his forehead. Getting him to feed on milk and cod liver oil from a pen filler presented no problem and Bonzo, as we called him, grew into a fine strong hare. He was always extremely tame and confident with us, but was easily alarmed by any unusual incident or by strangers. He spent every day in an enclosure in the garden, sitting crouched and motionless in his form, regardless of the weather. At night we brought him in to run loose in the drawing room where he enjoyed hiding and playing behind the long curtains.

My father, who appropriated Bonzo as his own, used to encourage him to sit on his lap. Should strangers enter the room, though, Bonzo promptly took refuge under the sofa or behind the curtains and if the visitors were unaware that the 'potty Payns' had a tame hare, they were liable to imagine that they were seeing things when the hare's face with his long ears and waving whiskers appeared from under the furniture. Bonzo loved grapes and bananas and when he thought it was time to be given some, he ran to the dining room door and stood there expectantly until one of us fetched him the fruit. But alas, he had an infernal temper and if he did not immediately get what he wanted, he was liable to bite and growl like a small dog; usually he was gentleness itself.

At bedtime the hare was put on the landing in a large wooden box crammed with green food and various vegetables. There he spent the long night hours eating his way through these delicacies. By morning little was left.

When Mother had her early morning tea, she let Bonzo out of his box and he immediately ran into the room, jumped on the bed and demanded a saucer of milky tea before burrowing under the eiderdown and going off to sleep there. Sadly this charming animal also met a violent end when a stray dog broke into his pen one day and killed him.

Much later, indeed only a few years ago, our animal family was augmented by the arrival of two small jet black lambs of the Welsh moutain breed which I acquired to help keep down the grass in the goose paddocks. We named them Marks and Spencer and they followed us about all day long demanding to be fed some titbit. If they were not given something, they were liable to give us a far from gentle thump in a painful place with their incipient little horns.

Mother doted on them and visited them daily with biscuits and lumps of sugar. On one occasion, when she had been ill in bed for some time, she asked how they were and said how much she would like to see 'the dears'. Why not I thought. I went down to the garden and calling Marks and Spencer from their enclosure, took them into the house where they followed me without hesitation up the stairs and into my mother's bedroom. There they stood with their forefeet on the bed, while she stroked their noses and gave them lumps of sugar. In the end they became too big and boisterous, and we sent them to Banham Zoo.

Although they cannot really be classified as pets, nor, except in a few cases, as family friends, I feel nonetheless that this would be a good point at which to introduce a group of birds which provided me and many other people with immense pleasure, and which occupied a very large part of my spare time over a period of more than twenty years. They were a collection of pinioned water fowl — wild geese and ducks and a number of waders that I kept at liberty in the garden.

Before the war, I kept at Hartest a small flock of water fowl — mallard, shoveller, teal, tufted duck and wigeon , some of which my friends or I had wing-tipped while out shooting, but most of which I had hatched from wild taken eggs. As the garden was not then well fenced against predators I suffered a number of losses from raiding cats and foxes, but I had great pleasure from the birds and was beginning to learn how to hatch and rear them and how to maintain them successfully from, as it were, the cradle to the grave.

While I was away in the army, my flock was gradually reduced to two dissimilar birds, a teal drake and a shoveller duck. I was told they had mated and that the duck had laid a clutch of eggs from which, surprisingly, two ducklings (a duck and a drake) hatched. With great skill Mother managed to rear them and I saw them while home on leave. Later, the duck disappeared, but the drake survived for a time and eventually died and was preserved. I was able to exhibit this remarkable specimen, which showed strong plumage characteristics of both parents, at a meeting of the British Ornithologists' Union, where it aroused much interest, being a previously unknown hybrid. The skin is now in the Harrison Zoological Museum at Sevenoaks.

With the idea of starting another water fowl collection after the war I began to fence in about an acre and a half of the garden to include two ponds, all the lawns and shrubberies and a good deal of what had become, as a result of war-time neglect, a wild garden. The entire area had to be enclosed within a six foot high chain link fence to keep out foxes and other predators, and to prevent inmates from wandering away.

All this was duly accomplished and within two years I had built up one of the first water fowl collections in the eastern counties. It was to survive for more than twenty years. At its peak, it comprised nearly thirty different species of geese and ducks, as well as a number of oyster catchers, curlews and other waders. This lively, diverse and many hued collection was a constant joy to me and gave great pleasure to many people who came from far and wide to see it.

When one day I was asked by a visitor — and it was a question which was often put to us — how many birds and beasts we then had in the collection, Mother and I estimated that we had, that day, more than one hundred and forty mouths to feed — those of geese and ducks, curlews and oyster catchers, a lapwing, a crippled black-headed gull, Reeves and other pheasants, red-legged and grey partridges, bantams, rabbits, ferrets, two dogs, two sheep, two budgerigars — and a tortoise; quite a little Noah's Ark.

Where the waterfowl collection was concerned it was my aim to keep and to try to breed from those species of ducks in which the males had particularly handsome plumage, such as mandarins, Carolinas, falcated teal and so on, or species from the Southern Hemisphere in which the drakes and ducks kept their bright colours throughout the year, having no eclipse dress as do our northern species. Among the exotics my favourites were always the Bahama pintail, the Chiloe wigeon and the striking little Brazilian teal.

Most of the wild geese, too, were to treasured for their shape and colouring and for their delightful wild voices, while the waders were always much admired, particularly the curlews, stately and deliberate in their movements — and the oyster catchers which were always busy, constantly probing the lawns in search of worms and leather jackets, and liable to burst suddenly into a chorus of piping trills, accompanied by excited runnings to and fro.

As a naturalist, I had endless pleasure from watching my birds about their daily activities as they paddled and dived on the ponds or foraged for insects and grubs on the lawns and flowerbeds. On a winter's night as I lay snugly in bed I could hear the voices of the geese and ducks and curlews which were carried through the open window — the quacking of the mallards, the whistle of wigeon and shrill pip pip of the teal drakes, punctuated by the sudden clamour of the geese; a chorus of voices that carried me away in spirit to some Scottish lochside or estuary.

Looking after this varied collection occupied a good deal of my time. The geese and ducks needed two feeds a day and in severe weather the ponds had to be kept clear of ice, and the birds protected from cold winds. The waders had to be taken under cover in frosty weather, or their toes were liable to become frost bitten; they also needed more animal protein than the waterfowl, relishing a mixture of cheese, raw meat and hard boiled egg.

In spring and summer I was kept busy searching for the ducks' nests, for in captivity wild ducks generally prove to be poor mothers and their eggs have to be hatched under bantams or in incubators. This was a fascinating but also at times most frustrating business, the mother ducks being most skillful at concealing their nests and also in approaching them by devious ways when they went to lay or to incubate. Some individuals teased and bamboozled me for days.

Waterfowl in captivity vary greatly in temperament; some always remain shy and wary of human beings, even those they know well, while others soon become tame and confiding. Some of ours were delightfully trusting and a number of the ducks and waders, which were free to roam where they liked in the garden, often came into the house and pottered about there. One Carolina duck took to laying her eggs in an armchair and a pintail drake, which became imprinted on me, used to walk up two flights of stairs to my work room where it would settle down and go to sleep beside my chair like a dog. A curlew that had been very ill, spent most of one winter sitting by our fireside. By the spring it had recovered.

One of my wild geese was quite a celebrity in East Anglia. He was a Greenland white-fronted gander which I had wing-tipped during a shooting holiday in the Hebrides. Within days of his capture he was contendedly eating soaked bread and dog biscuit, often taking it from my hand. He quickly settled down when turned out into the garden, and in time became as tame and friendly as a dog. Though I found him a mate, he took little interest in her, preferring the company of human beings.

At that time I was doing a good deal of lecturing on wild

life subjects, to field and social clubs, Women's Institutes and so on, as well as acting as a WEA tutor, and I often used to take Isla, as the old goose was called, as one of my props. He seemed to enjoy travelling in the car with me, sitting on the front seat and turning his head from side to side as though looking out at the view and chuckling to himself with apparent pleasure. He was a smash hit with audiences of all ages, being quite prepared to let small children embrace and stroke him. I noticed that he soon seemed to know when my talk was coming to an end, whereupon he stood up on tiptoe, flapping his wings and uttering that beautiful musical cackle which has earned the white-fronted goose the popular name of "laughing goose".

Isla had a number of other winning ways. He liked to lie down in front of the garden hose and let the water run into his open beak and over his back while he chuckled contentedly to himself. When we had tea in the garden, he always came and sat down beside us, talking quietly to himself and pecking up any bits of cake we dropped for him. Although he was adult when I rescued him, he lived with us for another twenty-five years, and never ailed until one morning he was found dead with his head tucked under his wing. We missed him as much as if he had been a human friend.

7

SUFFOLK UNSULLIED — THE BLISSFUL YEARS

The Suffolk of my childhood and early youth, the Suffolk of the 1920s and right on into the next decade, was a wonderfully beautiful and tranquil place when compared with what it has since become. It was also a naturalist's paradise. The countryside itself and people's way of life there, including farming customs and practices, had remained almost unchanged for one hundred years or more. The bulldozer and the agrochemist, those twin plagues of our modern countryside, were yet to appear on the scene.

Although, in the years immediately following the end of the Great War, farming was going through one of its periodic recessions, the farms were still the backbone of the village community. Indeed, most of our Suffolk farmyards were still examples to the life of the scenes portrayed in previous centuries by artists like George Moreland, Stubbs, the Herrings or the brothers Smythe of Ipswich.

Mixed farming was universal, with livestock an essential part of the economy of most arable farms and there was none of the ugly monoculture so prevalent today when many farms grow nothing but barley and sugarbeet and carry no livestock at all. In those days cows still grazed under the apple trees in farm orchards, the long faces of cart horses still looked out over the half doors of their stables and there was often an orphan lamb or two in a pen on the farm lawns.

The warm, dark old barns and outbuildings — many of them thatched, some in disrepair — were still full of young calves or of sows with litters. Ducks swam on the horse ponds and a motley collection of turkeys, geese and chickens foraged happily in every stack yard. In summer, the doors and windows of farmhouses stood open all day long and if for any reason a visitor called at a farm house it was often to find the place deserted and unguarded, except for the dog asleep in its kennel by the back door; the farmer and his wife were away in the fields, busy about their affairs with no thought then of robbers or vandals to send them hurrying home.

The old four course farming system was still followed everywhere, with a white straw crop — wheat, barley or oats — interspersed with beans, grown for the farm horses, or red clover for stover and to put nitrogen into the land, and for winter feed, fields of swedes or mangolds which were stored until needed in great earth clamps. Chemicals were little used, it was all farmyard manure which had been carted out throughout the year and piled in great heaps somewhere on the farm to be spread on the stubbles and ploughed in during the winter.

Some of the larger farms maintained flocks of folded sheep which were moved about to graze on old meadow land and on the fields of white turnips grown for them. We seldom went out on the roads without meeting one of the flocks as it was being driven from one pasture to another, the sheep and their bleating lambs flowing over the whole highway like a white tide, urged on by the shepherd and his dog. We never minded being held up in this way for five minutes or more as the flock went scampering past, for it was all part of our placid rural life.

Part of the regular tackle employed on many farms then were the great iron hurdles on wheels which were used instead of wooden hurdles, to fold sheep and cattle, or to block gaps and gateways. We often met them too on the highway, being towed by a horse in a long line, chained one behind the other, as they were moved from one pasture to another, the ringing and clattering of their iron wheels audible from afar.

A flock of the big black-faced Suffolk sheep, much used for

crossing with other breeds, was often folded on fields near my home and I spent many an hour gossiping with the shepherd and sometimes helping — or hindering — him as he worked, moving the wooden hurdles and hammering them into the soil with a crowbar, or thatching the sides of the fold with straw before lambing time.

His companion was an Old English sheepdog, the only one of that gentle breed that I have ever seen working, and I used to watch in admiration how sometimes, when the shepherd wanted a certain ewe singled out from the flock, the dog seemed somehow to know which one was wanted and would even gallop over the backs of the close packed flock until he reached and could separate the desired beast. I wonder if there are now any dogs of the Old English breed still working with sheep?

How quiet our countryside was in those days, with few aeroplanes roaring overhead, little motor traffic on the roads and no tractors clanking and grinding about the fields by day and night, all of which now combine to drown the simple sounds of nature. We could still hear the songs and calls of the birds, the skylarks overhead, rooks cawing in their nesting trees and the wailing of the peewits over the fields in spring.

The silence then would be broken only by the occasional rattle of a dog-cart or tumbril on the turnpike, or the voices of men working in the fields, or of a cowman calling in his cows to be milked. The horse drawn farm implements — grasscutters, drills, harrows and corn binders — made very little noise when compared with the roar of the modern combine harvesters, and of the vast tractors now in use everywhere.

Another sight and sound to which country people of my generation would doubtless look back, as do I, with some nostalgia, was the muffled thump of hooves and jingle of trace-chains as the ploughing teams came home from their work on a winter's day, with each ploughman sitting sideways on one of his horses, sometimes smoking a clay pipe and leaving behind on the evening air a familiar country aroma of horse sweat, leather, tobacco and corduroy.

Another sight trawled up from among the memories of those

79

long past days is of the travelling stallion man, so familiar then on our country roads as he led his great Suffolk Punch from farm to farm to serve their waiting mares. The great horse made a splendid picture as it went by, snorting and pounding, its glossy chestnut coat gleaming, the coloured tapes that decorated its mane and tail waving in the breeze.

Although a few tractors were beginning to appear — they were paraffin driven and always known by their trade name of Mogul, with the emphasis on the first syllable — horses were still universally employed on the farms and on many of them, for instance at my old family home at Somerton Hall, it was quite usual to see half a score of Suffolk Punches being turned out to graze after work on a summer's evening. I always delighted in watching them as they galloped about, with tails in the air, their bright coats aglow against the background of green grass and green hedges.

Those hedges and their innumerable hedgerow trees dominated the landscape, providing it with so much of its beauty and variety. Hedges enclosing the arable fields were kept within bounds by regular trimming, it being common practice then for a farmworker to 'take a hedge' from the farmer and, in his spare time during the winter, to cut and lay it neatly, keeping for himself the straight hazel and ash sticks to use as bean supports in his garden, the remaining branches being bound up as faggots.

But, for every well trimmed hedge there were many others, particularly those protecting the old meadows where the farm horses and cows grazed, which had been left to grow unchecked for years; and what tremendous hedges they were, ten feet or more in height and sometimes as wide, they were largely made up of hawthorn, hazel or blackthorn, often with a rich mixture of dog rose, maple, elder and spindle. Old countrymen called the latter peg-wood, because the gipsies used its long straight stems to make the clothes pegs which they hawked round the villages from door to door.

On a sunny autumn day those old hedges were a wonderful riot of colour with the blue-black sloes and clusters of black-berries mingled with the scarlet of rosehips, the orange-red of field maple and crab apple leaves, and the tufts of fluffy grey flowers of wild clematis or old man's beard.

While some of those great hedges were not particularly old, and had been planted to give protection to livestock — we called them quick-fences because they were made up largely of quick growing hawthorn — most of them dated back to at least the Enclosures Acts of the seventeenth century. Others were far older, being relics of the primaeval forest from which the adjoining fields had long ago been claimed for agriculture. These ancient hedges were easily identified — and still can be where they have survived — by the number of woodland plants such as primroses, bluebells, violets and wood anemones which still grew on their banks.

The economy of the villages also benefitted from the wild harvest provided annually by those huge hedges. In autumn, we all sallied forth to gather the elderberries and sloes for making into wine and sloe-gin and the crab apples for jelly, while huge quantities of blackberries went into jams and puddings.

No sooner, too, had the corn harvest been brought in, than the women of the village turned their hands to another free harvest — gleaning the fallen ears of wheat and barley left behind on the stubble fields. A good gleaner could fill her store shed with enough corn to support her chickens through much of the year. Gleaning is now a thing of the past as the ploughs are sent in to tear up the stubbles almost as soon as the combines have left the fields.

Incidentally, here are some little snippets of ancient rural lore which seem worthy of record. My grandmother Hale, who was born in 1862 and lived to the age of ninety-one, used to tell us how in her childhood at Walsham-le-Willows, on every farm the labourers used to nominated one of their number as 'Lord of the Harvest', responsible for organising all the work in the harvest field from the cutting of corn — still done then with scythe and sickle — till it was safely stacked. A green bough was always tied to the tail of the last wagon load taken in, and nobody was allowed to start gleaning anywhere in the parish until the church bells were rung to show that harvest was complete. Were these, I wonder, just local customs?

Many of our old meadows were just as beautiful as the great hedges which enclosed them. They too had lain unchanged, though not neglected, possibly for centuries; they were cut every summer for hay and grazed irregularly during the rest of the year by the farms animals.

Those dear Suffolk meadows of my childhood — how many happy hours I spent in them in spring, searching for larks' nests — for the larvae of the drinker moths and particularly for the hairy woolly bears which, if I kept them in glass jars and fed them on dock leaves, would later turn into the splendid scarlet, chocolate and white tiger moths that so delighted my childish eyes — as indeed they still do if I am lucky enough to find one asleep on a tree trunk or wall.

What hours too I used to pass on hot summer days, just lying in the tall grass of those same pastures before the hay cutter came round. There, half hidden in a rippling sea of grasses, richly spangled with the white stars of bull daisies and the gold of buttercups, I was in a private world of my own. Against the blue sky I could follow the dancing flight of a host of butterflies — blues and heaths, browns and coppers, ringlets and the curious skippers with their club like antennae and swift darting flight, while my ears were filled with the chirruping of the grasshoppers, many of which leapt fearlessly onto my clothes and hands.

Naturally I came to know most intimately the five old meadows that lay close about my home. They were typical of their kind, old pasture land, rich in flowers, protected by great hedges and hedgerow trees. Between two of them grew a particularly fine group of horse chestnut trees, the branches of which swept down almost to the ground. Small boys delighted to scramble and swing among their branches and courting couples enjoyed their shade on a hot summer's day. One meadow in particular became, in spring, an absolute carpet of green-winged orchis and cuckoo flowers, followed a few weeks later by great sheets of cowslips and buttercups, something seldom to be seen nowadays in Suffolk.

Yet even when at their best in spring or summer, the old

farm pastures could never quite match in beauty or interest the low lying water meadows that then stretched for mile after mile alongside our Suffolk rivers and streams. They were always green and bright with flowers, with wide tracts of marsh and rushy bog, sometimes flooded in winter for weeks on end. Farmers relied on them to provide grazing for their cattle in summer when the upland meadows became dry and short of keep.

The streams that meandered through them were clear and unpolluted, and seldom disturbed by man. Here they ran swiftly between steep banks, there rippled over gravelly shallows where clumps of rush and arrowhead had taken root and great fans of yellow and white crowsfoot undulated in the current. On the banks scattered willows and alder trees grew, some of which — old and windblown — had fallen across the water, providing a convenient highway from bank to bank for the wild things. In summer thickets of hawthorns and wild roses spilled their cascades of white and pink bloom down almost to water level.

This combination of stream and water meadow, marsh and willow jungle, so characteristic of Suffolk river valleys in those happy days, provided a wonderfully varied habitat for birds and butterflies, flowers, fish and mammals, on which human beings had, then, made little impact. It was what we would now call an ideal natural ecosystem. Alas, all too little of it has survived pillage by farmer and catchment board.

Our little local brook, the Smithbrook, which flows past just below my home, can boast no water meadow or marsh, for its stony course has cut its way deep into the land and its steep banks are heavily wooded throughout much of its length.

But it is a fine place for small boys to play in, to paddle or to look for fossils, foxes or pheasants, though not to be compared in interest and beauty with the Glem, a delightful stream that winds its leisurely way down the neighbouring valley till it joins the River Stour at Glemsford. The Glem lay within easy distance of my home and by the time I had reached my early teens I must have explored every yard of its length from The Butts at Hawkedon village down to the water meadows by Scotchford Bridge at Stanstead. It was my happiest hunting ground. I knew all its moods and most of its secrets.

I knew where kingfishers dug their nest tunnels in the river banks, and all the small marshy places, sometimes no more than half an acre in extent, where snipe and mallard nested in spring and where the exotic-looking redshanks often droppped in to rest when on migration in spring and autumn.

At Boxted Wick there was a glorious wilderness of reed and sedge marsh, bog holes and flooded ditches, dotted with willow clumps and thorn trees, never drained and seldom grazed, where in summer I was always sure to find water-rails and sedge warblers, whitethroats, blackcaps, reed and corn buntings. as well as a pair or two of red-backed shrikes, now so rare in Britain, but in those days not uncommon on wasteland and railway cuttings.

I loved it all, but best of all I loved the stream for, like so many people, I have always been fascinated by running water.

The Glem was full of fish then and my small friends and I enjoyed paddling in its shallows and trying to catch by hand the minnows, millers-thumbs and gudgeon that concealed themselves in the sand and the crayfish that lived in the weed.

Sticklebacks were plentiful and I used to take some of them home to be released in one of our garden ponds, or to be kept for a time in large jam jars. When I put two jars, each containing a male stickleback, alongside each other, it was entertaining to watch the two fierce little fish, gleaming scarlet and green in their impotent rage, as they tried to fight each other through the glass.

More orthodox sport could be had fishing with dough or worm for dace and rudd and most of the pools contained brown trout. These were descendants of some with which my father and Squire Poley had stocked the water between Hawkedon and Boxted many years before. My parent was always a keen fisherman and sometimes he took me with him on a summer's evening when he fished his favourite pools. We usually returned with a plump trout or two for supper.

The teeming wildlife found then in its river valleys was matched in numbers, if not always in variety, throughout the

The old shop, Hartest, burned down during the Great War

James Payn, novelist, as a young man

The old Suffolk ......

. . . . . and the new

Partridge shooting garb, early 1900's. Father (centre) with friends at Somerton Manor Farm

A harvest scene, 1920's

Father and mother with friends, Biskra, Algeria

A foray after partridges for the Mess. Tunisia, 1943

The waders were always lively and interesting

At ease in the heather, Perthshire

Suffolk countryside. Its cornfields and meadows, its lanes, heaths, marshes and old deciduous woods were full of birds and butterflies in numbers which seem unbelievable today. All our so called common resident birds — finches, skylarks, thrushes, blackbirds, tits and wrens, yellowhammers, woodpeckers, partridges, owls and kestrels — really were common and widespread everywhere, as were most of our summer migrants. Warblers nested in almost every hedge and rough scrubby corner, conspicuous among them the whitethroats which seemed to enjoy dancing before us along the hedge tops, flashing their white outer tail feathers as if to ensure that we would recognise them. We were used to finding their fragile little nests of hay and horsehair built deep in nettlebeds, hence their local names of hayjack and nettlecreeper. Blackcaps and garden warblers sang in spinneys and shrubbery and the rattling song of the lesser whitethroats sounded all day long from the tall thorn hedges. To find the nest of the latter was a real achievement as they were so small and inconspicuous, built ten feet or more up in the leafy canopy.

Cuckoos were common and their voices — surely the most delightful of all the sounds of a country spring — echoed throughout the live long day across the fields and woods. It was nothing unusual then to see a group of five or six flying and calling together as the males chased a female in courtship flight.

Old country house gardens, being quiet and undisturbed, were particularly attractive to birds, and ours was no exception. In the garden itself, and in the fields which surrounded it, nearly fifty species nested regularly. In summer, swallows and martins flew in clouds about the house and its outbuildings; at least a dozen pairs of swallows built their mud saucers in the stables and lofts, the doors and windows of which were always left open to let them fly in and out. Much loved too, despite the mess they made, was the colony of martins which built under the eaves. They have been there in varying numbers throughout my lifetime. Nesting house martins are said to bring luck to a house; I think they brought luck and certainly happiness to ours.

Besides swallows and martins my particular favourites among our garden birds are wagtails and flycatchers, one or two pairs of which have always nested here. The wagtails choose the ivy on the barn wall for their nests and our pair of spotted flycatchers have, for many years, built in an old kettle put up for them in a montana clematis on the garden wall.

As soon as they arrive in early May the flycatchers appropriate the croquet hoops on the lawn as launching pads for sallies after insects; there they compete with our spruce little wagtails which call so merrily and dash with such grace and agility about the lawns throughout the long summer days. In those days, they, or one of our many pairs of hedge sparrows, frequently became the over worked foster parents of a voracious young cuckoo.

For me one other vivid memory of those long-past garden summers is of the steady stream of goldfinch families, all cheerful twitters and flashing black and gold wings, which came to drink and bathe amid the waterlilies on the front pond. Few come now.

During the 1930s a pair of nightingales nested in the shrubbery by the drive. The male bird charmed us and our visitors with its wonderful contralto music and later the parents brought their speckled young to forage in full view of our windows. Hawfinches, too, bred nearby and we found frequent evidence of their early morning raids on our pea vines.

The rarest and most interesting of our garden birds then was the pair of red-backed shrikes which bred for several summers in an old meadow, overgrown with thorn trees, just outside the kitchen garden. We saw them almost daily, for both birds used our tennis posts as look out stations from which they could swoop on passing bees and butterflies. Unlike some of our neighbours, we always welcomed the wood pigeons which strutted about on the lawns, and the stock doves and turtle doves whose sleepy purring voices were so much part of those summer days. Our ringdows as the Suffolk countryman calls the wood pigeon — the stock dove being blue rock — did us little harm and were always left unmolested.

We often saw sparrow hawks hunting in the vicinity and kestrels and little owls bred round about in hollow trees. The curious moaning nuptual song of the little owl, uttered as it sat at the entrance to its roost, sounded on all sides in March and April. A pair or two of barn owls frequented most farms, living in hollow trees or the old dark buildings, and we saw them on summer evenings drifting noiselessly about over the garden and the surrounding meadows. Green and great-spotted woodpeckers were frequent visitors. A pair of the former had their nest hole in a large poplar tree in the orchard and we often saw them breaking open the ant's nests along the bank of the pond, while in autumn great-spotted woodpeckers always knew when the hazel and filbert nuts in the kitchen garden were ripe, and we could hear the sound of their hammering as they broke open the shells of nuts wedged in the bark of the great oak tree which grows in the hedge there.

In those days Suffolk had much other wildlife besides its birds to interest and delight the avid naturalist which I had by then become.

There were few wild deer in the county and foxes were certainly not as numerous as they have since become, but the hounds usually found after a meet on Hartest Green and there was always a breeding earth in the steep banks of the stream below our house. Hearsay also spoke of badgers in the Glem valley though I never saw one, nor its tracks there, until after the Second World War.

Hares were common, running before our car headlights at night and a dozen or more were often included in the bag when we went shooting. Red squirrels were to be found in most of the local woods. Rabbits abounded and all the smaller mammals such as field mice, voles and shrews were common in hedge banks and spinneys, as were the stoats and weasels which preyed upon them.

Those of us who were sharp eyed and knew where to look, could still find the fragile grassy nests of the harvest mice in the tangled hedges but the best place to see those delightful mice themselves was when they came running out of the barley stacks at threshing time.

Bats were far commoner than they are today, particularly the pipistrelle and long-eared bats that flew in any fine summer evening about the garden and outbuildings. Sometimes one would find its way through an open bedroom window. This usually alarmed lady visitors who imagined, quite erroneously, that it was liable to get tangled up in their hair. It was certainly a trifle eerie to hear and feel the soft whiffle of wings as the bat went round and round in the darkness before disappearing again out into the night. A colony of the large noctule bat lived in some old elm trees just outside the garden and were often on the wing in summer long before nightfall.

Butterflies were, and still are, my second love after birds and since childhood I have enjoyed watching, rearing and sometimes collecting them as specimens. Until intensive farming methods swept away most of their habitat, butterflies really swarmed in our lanes and flowery meadows.

If on a sunny summer's day then, anyone walked down the old lane which runs past my home, the butterflies would rise literally in clouds from the grassy banks and verges. Some twenty-nine species — browns and blues, heaths and coppers, ringlets, orange-tips, skippers and hairstreaks among others — were to be found commonly or locally throughout Suffolk. The red clover fields which were such a feature of the farming scene always attracted hordes of cabbage whites, peacocks and tortoiseshells and in hot summers immigrant painted ladies and clouded yellows. In spring among the first on the wing were the brimstones, the males of a brilliant saffron yellow, the females of the palest pastal green, unique among British butterflies in their leaf like wing shape. They are among my favourite butterflies.

In a good butterfly year our buddleias and sedums would be covered with tortoiseshells and peacocks, while the migratory red admirals visited the asters and became drunk on the juice of fallen apples and plums.

There were many other interesting and beautiful insects to be studied and admired in the garden and beyond. Most conspicuous were the big green and black dragonflies which zoomed about the lawns in search of flies. They showed little fear of human beings, frequently settling with a rustle of gauzy wings on our arms or shoulders. In May and June the more fragile blue and black damsel flies emerged and performed their dainty nuptual dances around the flag irises. Their life span was sadly brief.

Cockchafers and the iridiscent rose beetles were usually plentiful but we saw very few of the handsome stag beetles. Every countryman was familiar then with the glowworm lights which appeared on summer nights in damp meadows and lanes. We had a small private colony in one of our grassy yards. I was always fascinated by their pale bluish lights and by the way in which, when I picked up one of the small insignificant looking females, her light would go out instantly. Few glowworms are to be seen these days.

During my early childhood the range of my forays and explorations about the local countryside had, of necessity, to be restricted to places within walking or cycling distance of my home. Even though they owned a car my parents did not often go far afield in it; few did, then, cars being such an unreliable means of transport. Most of our neighbours quite happily walked, cycled or went about in some kind of horse conveyance; farm labourers almost invariably walked to their work.

So, at least until I reached my early teens, much of my native Suffolk was, for me a *terra incognita*. But as I grew bigger I began gradually to spread my wings, cycling further afield and sometimes pressurising my family to take me by car to visit hitherto unknown places which sounded interesting.

As I have already recounted, my parents had long made it a practice in summer to take me, and any guests who might be staying with us, for picnics in Breckland or by the river at Brandon, that ancient town which straddles the Little Ouse between Suffolk and Norfolk. Breckland, or the Breck as it is usually called by those who visit it often, is that vast, desolate, sparsely inhabited region, in those days almost treeless but now heavily afforested, which extends — some 400 square miles of it — from just north of Bury St Edmunds right up into south west Norfolk. The word breck, not, I think, found in many dictionaries, is an ancient word describing land once under the plough but then allowed to revert back to the wild.

In the days in which I knew it best and explored it most frequently — the 1920s and 1930s — the Breck was still one immense open wasteland, bright in summer with purple ling and great sheets of yellow ragwort, with scattered clumps of broom and gorse, and acre upon acre of bracken, interspersed with stony flinty desert on which only lichens and stonecrops grew. There were also quite considerable areas of sand dunes; one relic patch of these dunes, now a nature reserve, can be found alongside the Newmarket road a few miles to the west of Brandon. Here and there, too, scattered over the Breck, were small attractive meres, brim full in winter, but quickly drying out under the summer sun. Coots and a number of ducks bred upon them.

Anyone standing near the Elveden crossroads and looking northwards could see the town of Brandon and the green line of the Ouse valley across a glorious open vista of purple, gold and brown, framed within the dark lines of the Scots pines which protected against wind and blowing sand, the few roads and what little cultivation was then attempted on that arid soil. The great forest which has now blotted out so much of that view had not then been planted.

From the moment I first saw it the old Breck enchanted me. I am by nature a lover of wildernesses, of marshes and heaths, fens and deserts and Breckland had so much to offer me then — a new landscape, new birds and new plants. The specialised wasteland birds, wheatears and stonechats, woodlarks, nightjars and red-backed shrikes were widespread and locally common; ringed plovers, usually seashore birds, nested in numbers on the stony tracks and sometimes even in root fields, as did the stone curlew or Norfolk plover. That weird semi-nocturnal wader, with its eerie wailing call, 'Willie Reeve', epitomised for me the beauty of the wilderness in which it made its home.

Crossbills bred in the belts of Scots pine, and even sometimes in pines growing almost in the streets of Brandon, but the most exciting birds to my young eyes were the Montagu's harriers.

A pair or two of this now rare British breeding bird came every year at least up to the last war, to try and rear young on the Breck. They nested with varying success — for their eggs were much sought after by collectors — in the vast expanse of heather and whin to the south of the Ouse. I never felt that a day there was complete unless I had seen a harrier — and particularly the lovely black and grey male bird — sailing about over the heather.

Much of the Breckland flora is, like its birds, of the highly specialised steppe type, stunted and insignificant as a result of the arid conditions, constant grazing by rabbits, and battering by the wind blown sand. It is, I believe — for I am no botanist — of the greatest interest, with a considerable number of rareties and a few species found nowhere else in Britain. An old cousin of mine, a noted expert, went into raptures over what he found there during a morning's ramble and though I could not muster much enthusiasm for the various catchflys, speedwells and medicks he showed me, I could appreciate the common but eye catching flowers like viper's bugloss, evening primrose, scarlet poppy and the various clovers which added, in their season great sheets of colour to the Breckland scene.

I recall, too, how irritated my parents were at the profligate way in which my cousin, Colonel Arthur Payn, scattered the detritus of his botanical discoveries inside the car and all over the house when we finally got him home.

I believe that some of the Breckland species of moths are also of the greatest interest, but I never studied them myself. Butterflies were plentiful and there I made my first acquaintance with the curious grayling, a creature of the most arid, sun scorched terrain.

One of the more remarkable of Breckland spectacles in those days was the quite incredible number of rabbits which somehow managed to find a living in that inhospitable waste. There must have been many thousands of them, and their huge townships, dug in the sandy soil, were to be seen everywhere.

It amused me to take people who did not know the region to a long shallow valley not far south of Brandon, in order to show them how, as we appeared over the top of a slight ridge, the whole ground ahead of us seemed to be moving, as hundreds of feeding rabbits — many of them black, sandy or piebald — made for the safety of their warrens. That valley has long been covered by fir forest.

In former days rabbits were farmed for their meat and fur in wired-in warrens on many parts of the Breck, and in Brandon there was a flourishing business that made felt from rabbit fur for the manufacture of hats.

It is a tragedy that the old Breckland, a region unique in Britain, no longer exists except in small fragmented patches. Few people of my generation, and certainly few naturalists, could ever have imagined that a great gloomy forest, supporting a far smaller and less interesting fauna and flora, would one day swallow up the glorious expanse of beauty, light and colour which we loved so well.

Long before I was allowed to drive the family car, I had from time to time, in summer, undertaken the long cycle ride across Suffolk to watch the birdlife of its coastal belt, then largely neglected except by a few local bird watchers. I had a number of convenient bases there; at Felixstowe I could stay with an uncle and aunt and explore the Deben valley and the shore of the River Orwell by the old Dooley. Felixstowe was a good place, too, for butterflies and moths. I also got to know the deserted beaches and sea pools at Shingle Street where my cousin Claude Hughes had found the pine hawk-moth in the nearby forest. Some years later I spent two happy holidays staying with friends at Greyfriars, a large house perched right on the cliffs between Dunwich and Westleton and a wonderful place from which to study the local nightjars and stone curlews.

But Covehithe was my favourite haunt. I used to cycle over occasionally to stay for a day or two with a farm labourer and his family in one of those red brick cottages within a few hundred yards of the sea. I still recall with amusement how shocked I was at first to discover that the son of the house, who had been turned out of his bedroom to make room for me, was an ardent poacher. Over the tea cups he used to regale me with tales of his prowess in outwitting the Benacre keepers on dark winters' nights in order to acquire a brace or two of Sir Thomas Gooch's pheasants. At the age of fourteen I was already a keen game preserver, but in this case I diplomatically kept my feelings to myself.

How that coastal belt, the strip some ten miles wide running northwards from Ipswich to Lowestoft, has changed since those days. There was then far less cultivation, with great areas of heathland where Montagu's harriers still bred, more marshes and meres and, almost up to Lowestoft, much real breckland with its specialised bird life, similar to that in the west. On the coast the breck areas were always called sandlings, and were extensively grazed by flocks of sheep. There were also many small woods and marshes, ideal for the bird life which swarmed in them.

It is the beaches, though, which have altered most. Those between Southwold and Kessingland were far more overgrown with vegetation than they are today. Erosion by the sea did not then seem such a threat and several colonies of common and little terns nested on the beach in perfect safety from sea and man, for in those days, even in high summer, it was unusual to see anyone walking on the beach. Nightjars actually nested in places in the rough herbage just above high-water mark and it was near Easton Broad that I found my first nighjar's eggs. There, also, I saw my first bearded tits, while pheasants and partridges were regularly found feeding and dusting on the shingle. Ringed plovers were common but I do not remember ever seeing any oystercatchers there.

All in all, because of its variety of habitat and proximity to the sea, the Suffolk coastal belt has always been — and still is today — a far better area for wildlife than the highly farmed centre and west of our county.

8

ON STUBBLE AND HEATHER —
SHOOTING IN SUFFOLK AND SCOTLAND

I should like to think that, up to now I have played a reasonably useful role in life and that my various activities have brought pleasure and some benefit to others. Nonetheless, my life has been dominated by four main interests — the study of natural history, foreign travel, dogs and shooting.

They are placed in that order only because, for me, the first two are so closely linked, while gundogs and game shooting are part and parcel of each other. It would be difficult for me to have to decide which of the four have given me the greatest pleasure throughout my life.

I like visiting foreign lands, not only to see interesting and historic places and people, but also to study their flora and fauna. In the same way, most forms of shooting involve the active participation of a dog, or dogs, and to me the enjoyment of the one depends to a high degree on the presence and performance of the other. Some of the happiest days of my life have been spent here in Britain, and occasionally overseas, with a dog and gun in the company of congenial friends.

For more than sixty years shooting of one sort or another has been one of my chief relaxations. It is part of my heredity. My Hale grandfather considered shooting second only to coursing, while shooting and fishing were, with gardening, Father's main outdoor pleasures.

How clearly I recall, from my earliest days, the bustle and excitement as Father prepared to go off for a day's shooting. He was dressed for the part in typical late Edwardian garb — stiff collar, Norfolk shooting jacket with a leather patch on each shoulder, tweed knickerbockers or thick cord breeches, leather boots, leather gaiters reaching to the knee, and all topped up by a flat cap, the familiar gor-blimey, which was the invariable head gear of the countryman of those days.

Then there was the gun in its canvas sleeve, the bulging cartridge bag, the whistle on its lanyard and the leash to control the canine partner of the period; this, as I recollect, was either Jock, a fat black and white spaniel, or Nep, a chocolate coloured retriever. Ever since Father had appeared in his shooting clothes, they would have been dashing about the house with tails wagging and eyes on stalks, sending the rugs flying in all directions.

I can see Father now, standing on the front doorstep, watch in hand, moustache bristling, as he peered anxiously up the drive until, with much ceremony, George Pettit, our chauffeur/gardener, who also acted as Father's loader, appeared at the wheel of the large green Wolseley. Father kissed Mother, gave me a pat on the head, checked that all his accoutrements were safely aboard, and drove away.

Throughout that afternoon my excitement mounted as the time for his return drew near. Down in the hall or waiting on the doorstep, I listened for the sound of the car or looked eagerly for its headlights. At that time there were very few other cars about in our neighbourhood, and the first to appear would almost certainly have been his.

Father emerged, often wet and muddy, and sometimes cross if the day had gone badly, and made a rapid bee-line for the dining room in search of a large whisky, while the wet dog was left in my charge to be dried with a bath towel and given his dinner.

Next, there was the supreme ceremony of watching the laying out of the game. If Father had been shooting somewhere as a guest, there would be only the customary brace of birds — pheasants, partridges or wild duck. The handsome mallards, with their glossy green heads and curly tail feathers, were always my favourite, as they were laid out to cool on the larder floor. If Father had been shooting on his own ground there would generally have been a much larger bag to be inspected — pheasants, partridges, hares, rabbits and pigeons and occasionally a beautiful woodcock, to be admired and carefully stroked by childish hands.

The period covered by these first recollections of my father's shooting days was a comparatively short one, for I was initiated into the proceedings at a very early age. At first I was taken out by Mother or my nanny to watch events from the comfort and safety of the family car, and a little later was allowed to stand by Father during a drive or join the line when partridges were being walked-up in September.

Soon I was given the more useful if arduous task of acting as anchor man for Father's young Labrador, Trick. Like all the Payn dogs, Trick was highly enterprising, with a marked tendency to run-in or to chase hares. To check, to a certain extent, this undesirable tendency, Father hit upon the idea of attaching me to the dog — not, be it noted, the other way round. The results were predictable; at the age of seven or eight I was still a small, light child, while Trick was big and strong. Inevitably I spent a fair proportion of every shooting day being dragged, bumpety-bump, across plough and stubble and through many a bramble thicket, while Father's bellows to 'Hold that blasted dog, can't you boy?' echoed across the countryside. Any other child might well have acquired a lifelong aversion to shooting and gundogs as a result of such activities, but on me it all had an entirely opposite effect and I became, and have remained, a confirmed addict of both.

Before very long I was promoted from the role of beater to being allowed to join in at the end of the line of grown-up guns with my own little 4-10 gun; at first this had to be carried unloaded, and I pretended to fire at the coveys while Father watched to see that I did not point the gun dangerously at man or beast, and that I always went through the motion of unloading before getting over a gate or through a hedge. Such strict training is seldom, I think, practised by parents today — and more's the pity. I think that it made me a very safe gun, unlike some, of all ages, who are to be seen in the shooting field today.

I have heard some of my contemporaries, the safest of shots, recall being sent home in disgrace and *coram publico* by their father because they had fired a dangerous shot. Fortunately I was spared such a humiliation, though I once saw it happen to an adult gun on a Scottish grouse moor.

I shot my first partridge almost exactly sixty-five years ago. In the 1920s the partridge was widespread and usually plentiful on most Suffolk farms, and it was the custom for shooting parties to walk-up the coveys in early September before the stubbles were ploughed and the birds became wild. Bags of fifteen or twenty brace by three or four guns were then commonplace and keepers believed that the coveys flew better in October when driving started, if a few shots had been fired at them earlier on.

Unless it was a Sunday, Father invariably sallied forth on the first of September, alone or with one or two friends, in search of a few partridges for the larder; the next morning a brace of young birds, cold and roast, would have been waiting for us on the breakfast table.

I carried on this excellent custom up to 1940, but since then there have seldom been enough stubbles or enough partridges, to make it worthwhile going out after them, though, I still think the best way to eat my first August grouse is cold for breakfast. It must, of course be a young bird.

I recall clearly some of the old friends who shot regularly with my father. There was Colonel Booth from Hawstead, who always drove over to Hartest in a wagonette, accompained by his gardener and a very small black retriever with a docked tail. His horse had to be stabled with us during the day and this was an added pleasure for me as I had not, at that time, been allowed a pony of my own. The day usually ended with me being led round our stable yard bareback on the colonel's horse, by his friendly factotum.

Then there was the Revd. Beilby Oakes, rector of Hawkedon

and one of Father's oldest friends with whom he had shared a shoot for many years. Mr Oakes was a fine shot and always used expensive cartridges with all-brass cases which did not suffer in the wet like the cheaper brands. We small boys vied with each other to stand by the rector during a shoot in order to gather up the empty cases; one or two of them are still lying about in the outbuildings here. Father used to get very cross with his old friend, because he liked to wear a white panama hat when out shooting in September and Father said that it scared the birds.

Another friend of long standing who also exasperated Papa when out shooting was Bernard Gaussen of Thurston End, who talked at the top of his voice while shoots were in progress and, of course, further alarmed the birds. Mrs Gaussen was a French princess, one of the Murats, and their house at Hawkedon was a veritable museum of Napoleonic relics.

A neighbour of ours, one of our closest and dearest friends, was Major Arthur Magan of the Dublin Fusiliers. He and his wife lived at Stowe Hill, a house only a short distance up the road. He was a delightfully eccentric man, very fond of enteraining and we went there many times during the course of the year to play tennis or bridge, or to dine, or to help thin out his young rooks on the twelfth of May.

Arthur Magan loved shooting and dogs and owned a series of Irish water spaniels, all of them called Biddy. It was said of him that when out shooting one day he left his car for a moment with the engine running, and with one of the Biddys sitting on the front seat. Somehow the dog managed to jolt the car into gear and away it went until brought to a halt in the nearest hedge.

On another occasion, he asked an Irish friend to stay and to shoot and at the end of the day, while cleaning his gun in the billiard room, the visitor accidentally discharged his piece through the ceiling and very nearly hit his hostess in her room above. The episode caused considerable amusement among the neighbours and Magan soon joined in the hilarity.

This train of thought leads me to believe that grown-ups were far more jolly and amusing in those days than is the case now. Father and his friends seemed always to be laughing, joking and playing pranks on each other. They had fewer worries then in a Britain and a world which was so much more peaceful and secure.

Another of our neighbours, just across the river in Essex, was Archie Campbell-Lambert, a big land owner and farmer. The Lamberts have long been among our closest friends. Archie, too, loved shooting and was the first of my father's friends to ask me out on my own. Many happy days did I have shooting with him at Foxearth and Liston in the years before, and just after, the war. He was a great character. He always wore a stiff shirt and collar, even when playing tennis or shooting. His tennis racket was almost square, not the usual oval shape, and probably dated from the early days of the century.

His shooting lunches were justly renowned for their excellence but when I was younger and more energetic than I am now, I did not approve of their length. We seldom got back to lunch at Foxearth Hall before 1.45 p.m. Long after I was ready and raring to go the port was still circulating merrily and the cigars going at full puff.

I remember that, as dusk began to fall on a November day, Crissell the keeper would appear at the dining room window and call out to his master; 'Come you on out, Sir, that's gettin whooly dark'. So out we all trooped for one more partridge drive in which we could scarcely see the birds, let alone our neighbours, whose positions were marked only by the flashes of their guns. But what happy days they were, when English partridge coveys were still plentiful on our Suffolk farms.

Another local character who shot regularly with my father when I was a boy was TB Ambrose, who farmed at Cavendish. A fine cricketer and shot, he was later a member of the Hengrave Shoot in which I also had a gun. He always asserted that he had been shot three times by his father when out rabbiting, including twice in one day.

Memory now conjures up a Suffolk partridge drive in which I am acting as my father's cartridge carrier. He stands at the extreme end of the line and a young Tom Ambrose is one of three guns next to him on his right. Down the line, with the wind under their tails, a covey of eight partridges comes hurtling. Each of the three guns on the right — another was Alec Ritchie, our family doctor — takes his brace, leaving the last two to be disposed of by my father with another neat right and left.

At a guess, this little episode took place some sixty years ago and I am probably the only one left of those who made up the party that day, unless some of the beaters were boys of my age, and are still living.

My own shooting career began modestly enough, first with a Daisy airgun at the age of six, reinforced a little later by an ancient BSA air rifle, which a more affluent young friend passed on to me. With them I made life a misery for the local sparrows. My twelfth birthday was marked by a gift from my dear cousin, Arthur Payn, of a double-barrelled 4-10 gun which was to last me until at the age of sixteen my father gave me a Stephen Grant 12-bore. This was an old side lever gun with Damascus barrels, which served me well for a number of years until, when my father gave up shooting for good, I took over his pair of Beesley 12-bores. None of these guns was an ejector, but with practice I found I could load quickly enough not to be handicapped when birds were coming thick and fast during a drive.

With my new 4-10 gun I soon mastered the general requirements of shooting at moving targets and in due course shot my first partridge. This important event — the first milestone as it were — in my shooting career, took place in a clover field behind Somerton Hall. Little William Hunt our keeper, had taken me out alone in order to achieve it. Alas, this proved far more difficult than I had anticipated and despite heavy expenditure of ammunition I had failed to score by lunch time when, very dejectedly, we returned to the keeper's house, Fortune smiled later when, out of the first covey which we flushed from that clover field, I brought down the young bird that I was able proudly to display to Father when he came to collect me that evening.

I achieved my first pheasant some time later and with very much less effort for, I am ashamed to say, it was sitting in a tree. I was staying at Kelling in Norfolk, at a house which adjoined the Kelling Hall estate, a very fine shoot belonging to Sir Henri Deterding the oil magnate. His land absolutely swarmed with pheasants and a number used regularly to roost in a small spinney belonging to the house where I was staying. Having duly noted a cock pheasant going to perch there one evening, I crept out an hour or two later and, getting him nicely silhouetted against the moon, duly committed the fell deed and murdered him as he slept. There was a sharp frost that night and when I picked him up his tail was frozen as hard and solid as a spear.

Before the last war game shooting in Suffolk was very different from what it has since become. All shoots then were privately run; syndicates were unkown and most of those we met out shooting were close neighbours, yeoman and tenant farmers, doctors, lawyers, retired officers and a parson or two — a rather small circle who met regularly and frequently at all the local shoots. Strangers from outside, unless they were relations or friends staying with local guns, were comparatively rare.

It is interesting to note that shooting was then looked upon as the cheaper sport when compared with fox hunting; indeed, compared with the astronomical prices which have to be paid today for shooting rights or to join a shooting syndicate, things were very cheap.

Although I have done most of my shooting in southern Britain, and that chiefly in East Anglia, some of my happiest and most eventful days with a gun have been spent north of the Borders, in the Western Isles and particularly in the Highlands of Scotland. I first went north in the Autumn of 1933 when my good friend, Colonel Richard Meinertzhagen, invited me to stay with him and his family at Swordale in

Ross-shire. I was entranced by it all: I had never seen anything to compare with the beauty and wildness of the Highland landscape. Autumn was late that year and there was little snow except on the high tops. The glens were still aglow with the scarlet and gold of the rowans and birches, and the soft greens of the larches.

The weather was kind and almost every day I was able to roam afield with my binoculars, seeing so much that was new to me — new birds and beasts and plants, even new styles of agriculture. On the moors I saw my first coveys of grouse and my first blackcock. Blue hares, then in their winter coats, sat about in the heather like so many angora rabbits. Another new bird, a little cock merlin, gave me a perfect view as it flew by in pursuit of a pipit. Wandering down the glens with their rocky, tumbling burns, so different from my familiar Suffolk streams, I was able to watch the dippers swimming and diving underwater or admire a group of gooseanders as they flew by.

One day we went out in a fishing boat on the Dornoch Firth where we sailed close to noisy flocks of long-tailed ducks and velvet scoters, divers and margansers and were even lucky enough to see a peregrine falcon strike down a lapwing, my description of which was later published in *The Times*.

Then came the great day when I bagged my first grouse. A hare drive had been arranged, with a large number of guns taking part. Although he had stopped shooting grouse for the season, my host said that if one came near me, I was to take it. None obliged during the morning but later in the day an old cock with the wind behind it came sliding round the shoulder of the hill in front of me, putting on speed and curl on seeing the line of guns. Down it came to my shot, with a most satisfactory thump, almost on top of the next gun. My day was made.

It is interesting to recall that more than two hundred hares were killed that day and that they were all left in a heap for the crows and other scavengers because it was not, in those days, worth the expense of sending them to market. A friend of mine who has a moor in Aberdeenshire tells me that nowadays a party comes over every year from Holland to shoot his blue hares and pay for the pleasure. How times change!

That first visit to the Highlands of Scotland engendered in me a deep love of a beautiful region and of the 'sport' that it has to offer. Except for the hiatus created by the war, there have been very few years since in which I have not spent at least two or three weeks bird watching or shooting in those dear Highland hills.

Right up until the Second World War we in the south conducted our shooting operations in a far more spartan manner than we do now. There being no such things as Landrovers or other cross-country vehicles, we all walked everywhere, guns and beaters alike. On the bigger shoots, where the bag was likely to be one hundred and fifty or more head of pheasants, partridges and hares, a game cart of some kind was in use; it was usually a horse drawn wagon or tumbril, while most of the really big estates like Ickworth, Euston and Kilverstone, had handsomely painted game carts, drawn by ponies. Some were real antique pieces. Otherwise, all game bagged by smaller shooting parties was carried by the guns and beaters until it could be hung up in some convenient barn, or taken back to the game larder.

Unless it was the last day of the season or there was some particular reason why shooting had to take place on the appointed day — perhaps it was a boys' day at Christmas — nobody tried to shoot on a very wet day when sport would have been poor and far from enjoyable. As most of the beaters were employed on the estate where shooting was taking place, or came from the nearest village, if it were wet the shoot was simply postponed until the following day, or some other convenient day. When the weather started wet but seemed likely to clear up later, the shooting party often adjourned to the house to gossip, or play bridge, until a final decision was made whether to shoot or to go home. Today, with many beaters coming some distance by car, and with lunches often arranged at the nearest pub, shoots are not easily postponed and we are dragged out to shoot in the most appalling weather.

The beaters pay then was 5s (25p) for a man and 2s 6d (12½p) for a boy, but they also had a very substantial lunch and a bottle of beer each, and I can well recall the huge hampers of food that were packed and sent out from this house for the beaters. Many beaters came ‚out for the enjoyment rather than for the money, as indeed many of them still do, and some of them were practically professionals, spending the whole winter moving about from shoot to shoot. As they had often acted as beaters from childhood, many of them knew as much about the efficient running of a shoot, and took as much pride in it, as did the owner or his keeper.

Some of the guns with whom I shot in my youth were absolutely top class, — scarcely surprising since many of them shot three or four days a week throughout the season. One who particularly comes to mind was Tom Pearson-Gregory of Assington, said to be among the ten best shots in Britain at that time. Comparatively few people used double guns then and Pearson-Gregory liked to hold a spare cartridge in his left hand so that he could get off a third shot at a covey, having killed one or two birds with his first shots. He also held a lighted pipe in his mouth while shooting.

Some of the other fine shots whom I saw perform in Suffolk included Sir Christopher Magnay, a particularly good and graceful pheasant shot, Colonel Anderson of Langham, Sir Charles Rowley, Colonel Henry Lowry-Corry, Hugh Buxton and Lawrence Hyde-Parker; all were very good indeed, and so I think was my father, particularly at driven partridges. Nor must I forget Frank Roper of Lavenham. He and I served together for some years during the war both at home and in North Africa.

I saw Frank shooting on a number of occasions and always envied the quick, neat way in which he mounted his gun and killed his birds. He seldom seemed to miss and was a particularly dab hand at driven snipe. I was indeed lucky to have been able to shoot in such company. I learned a lot from them.

All those who shot regularly in those days knew and observed the etiquette and customs of the sport. They were also interested in and knowledgeable about the life and habits of game birds and beasts, knew how a shoot should be run and something about the problems that confronted gamekeepers throughout the year.

As virtually all shoots were privately owned or rented, their owners would have seen to it that no undesirable practices were allowed to creep in. There were, admittedly, tales of hunts which turned out bagmen before a meet, but certainly no such thing as instant pheasants would have been countenanced. No decent sportsman in those days would have thought of shooting pheasants which had been let out of a pen only a few hours before they were put over the guns, as has been known to occur nowadays.

I believe the modern shooting scene is becoming far too mercenary and commercialised. Surely, charging so much per bird or per brace shot is, in every way, thoroughly undesirable and liable to lead to skulduggery of one sort or another. It is also a pity that so many shoots find it necessary to sell let days to total strangers, in order to help their own finances.

We hear tales of how such guns will sometimes go to the extent of kicking some of their dead birds out of sight, before the pick up. This may be true, one cannot tell without personal experience. But I can well imagine it taking place in some pay-by-day shoots, about which there are many odd tales. At one such shoot I saw plenty of evidence of people who consistently fired at birds over their neighbour's head and at birds and hares at extreme range, quite unconcerned if they went away wounded. I actually saw one sharp-shooter kill a hen pheasant as she trotted through the line.

With so many individuals newly come to the sport, some with so little interest in, or knowledge of, the countryside and its wildlife, it is inevitable that we will meet some who do not know, or who choose to ignore, the accepted customs and practices of the shooting field. Our modern shooting world certainly has its faults.

Game shooting is also being spoilt, and getting itself a bad name, because of the vast number of hand reared pheasants being put down on some shoots. Generally such birds do not fly well. They are often over fed, over fat and over tame. As they are to be seen during the autumn in fields and lanes, and even in peoples' gardens, where they run about like chickens, the idea that they will become quarry when the shooting season starts quite naturally offends non-shooting people, and lends fuel to the anti-field sports lobby.

Furthermore, this practice of releasing, year after year, great numbers of pheasants which have been hatched and reared in game farms, and have never seen their natural parents, means that any stock surviving at the end of the season, is becoming less and less capable of hatching and rearing its own young in the wild. As a result, the existing strain of truly wild pheasants seems likely to become more diluted until eventually it dies out altogether, leaving the large, heavy game farm strains to dominate our shoots.

I do not wish to disparage game farm pheasants unduly, for after all they are the mainstay of most big bag shoots nowadays and can, when properly shown, fly well enough. Yet most shooting folk — and I am one of them — would much prefer to shoot the small, quick flying wild pheasant, still to be found in places, and particularly in East Anglia and Scotland.

While I was away from home during the war years, my thoughts naturally and often turned to Suffolk and to my shooting friends there. I received very little news of what was going on, indeed I lived in a complete void where Suffolk sport was concerned. The only pre-war shooting friend I met thoughout the whole period was Ben Finch-White, formerly of Pentlow. We met on top of Toukabeur, a rocky tableland overlooking the approach to Tunis. Ben was then a half colonel, commanding a regiment of the East Surreys. We had time only to exchange greetings before returning to the business of waging war.

When, finally, in March 1946, I came home to Suffolk, I had no idea what to expect in the way of past friends and past shoots, but I was determined to resume such of my past activities as was possible. In fact I was lucky. Cyril Fairhead, an old friend of many years, let me have again the shooting on Somerton Hall and the Baronet (Sir William Hyde-Parker) handed over the shooting on his Burton's Farm to Harold Ward, Colonel Archie Taylor and me. The summer of 1947 was, if I remember correctly, very wet and game was scare. Nonetheless, we were all very glad to get to grips with the few partridge coveys and even fewer wild pheasants that had survived.

Gradually things improved. For several years I went wildfowling on the Solway and in the Western Isles, being joined later by the Darley brothers, very old friends from Poslingford. Later, I took a half share in the Redgrave shoot, to which I introduced a number of new guns. So it has gone on. In the forty years or so since the end of the war, I have been given the opportunity to shoot as a guest of many good people who own or owned East Anglian or Scottish shoots. I have also been able to rent, for my own benefit and that of my friends, a number of small grouse moors north of the Borders. By so doing I have got to know a considerable number of sporting individuals, some of whom remain close and much valued friends both on and off the fields and hills where we first became acquainted.

I have lost touch with some, I have forgotten the names of others; worse still, long ago I ceased to enter their names — as was formerly my wont — in my game book. I regret it now, but it is too late to remedy. For that reason alone I have not mentioned by name in this memoir, which covers close on seventy years of my shooting life, any of my good friends who have shared those days with me. Those who may read this will, I am sure, know how much I enjoyed and valued the days I spent, both with and without a gun, in their company.

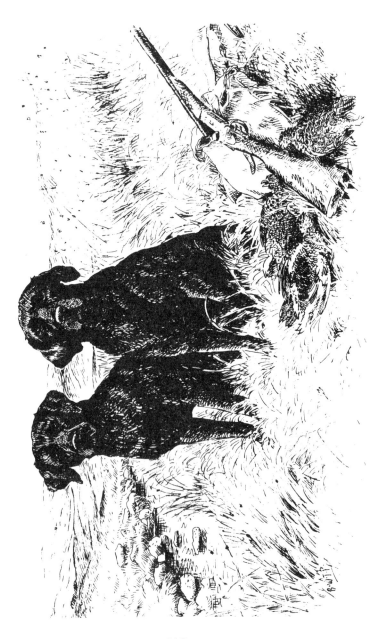

9

MY GOOD COMPANIONS OF BUTT AND BEN

I have a passionate love of dogs, inherited no doubt from a long line of dog loving ancestors. Few photographs are to be found of either Payns or Hales in which dogs of some sort do not figure prominently. As for myself, except for a period when I first joined the army, I have scarcely ever been without the company of a dog.

Grandfather Hale, as already recounted, kept a large kennel of greyhounds, as well as a miscellaneous collection of terriers and bulldogs. Father, whose chief outdoor recreation was shooting, naturally favoured gun dogs of which I can just remember Nep, a chocolate coloured retriever and Jock, a large black and white spaniel, with which I was regularly photographed.

Mother's love of dogs equalled my own and to a large extent our daily lives revolved round them. In my childhood she kept a number of Pekinese and Yorkshire terriers and one of the latter, 'Booty' by name, very nearly cut short my young life before it had really begun. The little dog had appointed himself my guardian, lying watch and ward all day by my pram. One day, somewhat over zealous, he jumped into the pram and lay protectively upon my face. I was, I have always been told, already purple in the face and close to suffocation before he was discovered and removed in the very nick of time.

Another of Mother's dogs, a large yellow and white pekinese called Ching, also fell from grace. After a number of years of blameless life, he took to lying in ambush at the bottom of the drive till the local children went past in the morning on their way to school. He then dashed out and gave their heels a nip. Mother became rather tired of having to hand out five shillings whenever an irate parent appeared waving a torn sock which might, or might not, have been Ching's handiwork. It became altogether too expensive and poor Ching had to go. He was accordingly packed off to Bayswater to live with a family friend who had always admired his good looks.

Once there Ching acquired a love for the Underground Railway. After breakfast every morning he set off, boarding an Inner Circle train and spent the day going round and round in it, only returning home, having alighted at the right station, in time for his evening meal. He became quite famous as the 'Underground Dog'.

I have owned — some might say I have been owned by — many dogs and except for about a year during the last war, I have never to this day been without one or more, almost all of them black Labradors. For me, life without the company and companionship of a dog would be scarcely bearable.

My first dog was a small Labrador called 'Trick'. He really belonged to my father but gradually I appropriated him as a friend and playmate. I remember his arrival well, for Trick was probably one of the few dogs in history to have been run over twice within an hour, by the same vehicle. He had been bred by my father's keeper at his cottage away in the fields at Somerton, so remote from all traffic that he would never have seen anything larger than a bicycle.

One of our neighbours, a farmer named Abbott, owned some land at the end of the lane which ran past our house, and visited it almost daily in his dog cart. He always drove like Jehu and on the first day of Trick's sojourn with us Mr Abbot went rattling past as usual. Trick dashed out barking furiously at this strange object and contrived to get his toes run over.

Rather sorry for himself, he limped away into the yard, but an hour or so later, as Mr Abbott came tearing back, Trick again rushed out and was again run over, though luckily he was not seriously hurt.

When he first came to live with us Trick and I were much of an age — he being rather less than a year old, while I was six. Soon he became my much loved and most devoted shadow, involved in every childish activity in which I was engaged. We went birds' nesting together, joined in the slaughter of rats and mice when stacks were being thrashed, swam in the stream in summer, went rabbiting and fishing; indeed there can have been few interesting occupations then available to a country boy and an active young Labrador in which we did not immerse ourselves.

Trick lived a long and happy life, dying, much lamented, at the ripe age of sixteen years.

I bought the first dog that I could really call my own when I was sixteen years and he was sixteen weeks old, and he cost me the huge sum of thirty shillings. He was one of the light, active Labradors I have always favoured and he proved to be one of the best workers I ever owned. I called him Whisky and owed him many of the shooting invitations which I then received. He had a fine nose, was an admirable marker, which a retreiver needs to be, and he was almost tireless.

The Labradors of my youth were usually huge, coarse dogs and many modern dogs are too large and heavy. All of those that I have owned or bred during the past thirty-five years have been smaller and lighter in build, and therefore much more active. They also tire less easily than the heavier type of dog.

I also favour bitches rather than dogs, despite the disadvantage of their seasons. I have a theory that bitches are easier to train and more biddable than the males. A dog works to please himself while a bitch works to please her owner or handler. It would, I think, be hard to find anything to match the single minded, uncritical love and devotion of a bitch for her owner, and all the more so if the bitch be a Labrador.

Besides Labradors, I also have a great affection for bull terriers and when the time came for me to join the army, I left Whisky, my thirty shilling Labrador, at Hartest and, as soon as I was able, acquired a small Old English bull terrier bitch. She was white with a black patch over one eye which gave her a rather comical look. I called her Minx, though she was usually known by the family as Minny. For two years she shared my army life. We trained together over the Dorset hills and on field exercises, and she served as a useful hot-water bottle, tucked up against my back as I slept in a wood or ditch.

At first she was very gun shy, but gradually I managed to break her of her fear of firearms and eventually she would sit quite happily on the turret of my tank while firing was in progress, unmoved by the bangs and recoils of a six-pounder gun.

Before that we had been involved in beach defence duties and while I was particularly glad to have her company at night when, as orderly officer I had to visit our sentry posts among the dunes, Minx preferred to hunt rabbits as I walked along, galloping about after them through the mine fields. Mercifully as they were anti-tank mines, she never exploded any.

Minx had two vices — alcohol and cats. Her fondness for alcohol became expensive. In the Mess, after dinner, when my fellow officers were enjoying their port, they had a habit of putting their glasses on the floor by their chairs. Minx soon discovered this alcoholic bonanza and crept round helping herself from any glasses within reach. Bellows of rage greeted the discovery of her depredations, while replacing the missing drinks played havoc with my Mess account. But she was worth it.

Like most bull terriers, she loathed cats and involved me more than once in embarrassing situations connected with them. Somewhere — I think it was in Swanage — I was walking down a street with Minx at my heel when she spied a black cat sitting on a doorstep. Like a flash she was away after the cat, which disappeared into its home with the dog in pursuit. When, a few moments later, I arrived breathless on the scene, absolute bedlam reigned. The cat was bounding round the room from table to chair, from chair to bookcase, and ornaments flew everywhere. The cat's owner was adding her screeches to Minx's excited yaps. Luckily the cat took refuge on top of a curtain rail and I was able to gather up my errant creature. The damage done was considerable.

Another incident involving Minx and a cat took place back in Suffolk after the war. A farming acquaintance was showing me over his land and Minx was taking exercise with us. As we walked home towards his house a very large black cat ran across the lane ahead and at once my dog took off in pursuit. 'I hope that isn't your cat,' I said to my companion. 'Don't worry,' he replied with a laugh. 'That old cat can look after himself with any dog.' Knowing Minx's capabilities, I kept my doubts to myself as we walked onwards, and when we reached the house my worst fears were realised, for there on the lawn sat Minx, with a smirk of self satisfaction on her face, and before her the corpse of the very dead black cat. All its owner could say was; 'Well, that is a rummun'.

One other recollection of that much loved and courageous little animal is worthy of record. Travelling down to Winchester by train one day during the war, I found myself sitting opposite Cyril Garbett, Bishop of Winchester, and later Archbishop of York. Minx was with me and she at once made friends with the bishop, who added to her interest by giving her one of his sandwiches. He told me that he also had a dog — a red setter — to which he was obviously much attached, and how one day when out for a walk with him she had caught a pheasant and he had had to smuggle it home under his coat for fear somebody might think he had been poaching. 'But,' he added, 'I wasn't really sorry because we hadn't anything very much in the larder that day.'

Minx adapted very well to army life, but when my regiment received embarkation orders in February 1943, I took her back to Hartest where poor old Whisky was nearing the end of his days.

Once overseas I began to look round for some sort of canine companion. The North African scene was not propitious. Most of the French farmers kept a pointer or two but otherwise the only dogs to be seen were the packs of great shaggy creatures which guarded the Berber villages.

They were very savage, attacking any stranger not on horseback or in a vehicle. Several of our men were badly mauled by them, so a warning was issued to the troops not to go out on foot unless armed. One evening the brigadier and I, when on our way to flight ducks by a small lake near camp, were set upon by a number of these great dogs and had to shoot two of them to prevent being savaged.

It was not until we moved to Italy that I found a suitable companion. Near a village just north of Rome, one of our HQ staff who was also a dog lover, mentioned to me that some sort of gun dog was hanging about the brigade cookhouse. It appeared to be starving.

When I had time to spare, I went to have a look and there found a large pointer dog with his nose in the swill tub. Lemon and white in colour, he had a very handsome 'Dismal Desmond' head and long ears: in truth he appeared to be all head, for he was not only thin but almost a walking skeleton. Bribed with a piece of bully beef, he followed me back to camp where my batman gave him a good meal and tied him up.

He settled down at once and was to share, with mutual affection and happiness, my army life for the next two years in Italy and France. Local Italian hunters told me that he was a Bracco — a kind of Italian pointer — and by the look of him, very well bred. I called him Brac.

Once we had put some flesh back on his bones he looked a very handsome fellow indeed, so much so that when, later, he walked at my heels about the streets of Paris, people often stopped and exclaimed 'Quel beau chien'. For some reason he disliked Italians intensely and was always a most efficient guard against those who would otherwise have pilfered from my tent or car. It was obvious he had been trained to the gun and we had many a happy and productive hour together after woodcock and partridges. He used to ride everywhere with me, standing in the back of my Jeep and was quite unconcerned by the heaviest shell-fire.

When I was demobbed in the spring of 1946, and left Paris, I gave Brac to Bernard de Billy, a French friend with whom I had had many enjoyable days' shooting, and who was another of the dog's admirers.

This brings me to the long line of black Labradors — bitches all — that have been my loving companions in butt and ben during the past forty years.

Just after the war it was difficult to get a good gun dog at anything like a reasonable price, but I managed to acquire a well bred bitch whose full brother was a field trial champion and had been exported to New Zealand. She was a dear, sloppy old dog but not very useful in the field. She 'dropped to shot', the only dog I have ever seen do so, and she retrieved dead birds lying in full view most efficiently, but if a 'runner' fell in the open and swiftly disappeared into a thick hedge or patch of brambles, she just stood and watched it go. Sadly, though perhaps fortunately for me, she died of distemper in early life.

Her successor was Trigger, bred from a long line of good workers. She was also highly intelligent and showed it when I collected the eight-week-old pup from the farm where she had been born. She sat very quietly on my lap as I motored home, but when we got there I discovered that she had been car sick on the way and had had the splendid idea of disposing of it all in one of my pockets. She was always slightly cross grained with other dogs, particularly when she thought she was guarding my possessions. She turned into an excellent worker and a good house dog and companion, being particularly devoted to my mother.

One of Trigger's escapades was much talked of as she was, I imagine, one of the few dogs ever to have stopped the 'Night Scotsman' train. My friend Colonel Bob Darley and I were travelling up to Scotland to shoot. At Euston we tied up our respective dogs — both black bitches — in the guard's van and told him the number of our compartment in case he should need to contact us.

We had been asleep for only a short time when there was a knock on the door and the sleeping car attendant announced that there had been a little trouble in the guard's van and the guard would be obliged 'if the gent whose dog is tied up in the corner will please go down there.' The train was then at a standstill.

Half asleep, I mumbled: 'There you are Bob, your old dog has probably been chewing the parcels'. To which Bob, equally sleepily replied: 'My dog isn't in the corner, that's where you tied Trigger up.'

Unfortunately this was true, so I had to get out of my warm berth, put on a dressing gown and make my way down the length of the now motionless train.

Arriving in the guard's van, I was greeted rapturously by Trigger and somewhat grumpily by the guard. I asked what had happened. 'Well Sir, said he, 'when their passengers have settled down the attendants like to come along here and have a chat and a cup of tea with me. Your old dog allowed them all to come past, but when they wanted to return she wouldn't let them go by.

'I am sorry about that,' I said, 'but they seem to have got back safely now. What did you do?'

'Oh,' he answered, 'I had to stop the train — I am in charge of it you know — and they all climbed out on to the track and got in again further back.'

Next morning, when I collected my errant animal, I had no hesitation in crossing the guard's palm with gold. I heard no more of the incident.

I bred a good litter of pups from Trigger, all of which went to shooting friends, except one bitch which I kept for myself. 'Zulu', as I called her, was a throwback, with a very thick wiry coat and a heavy plumed tail, an ideal wildfowling dog. She turned into a very steady old worker with a number of curious habits, and she thought I was God.

An instance of her remarkable memory comes to mind. One cold winter's day, with snow and ice on the ground, I was walking with her along the bank of a river on the chance of a shot at a duck. In due course I shot a mallard which fell into a wood on the other side of the river. Zulu swam across and gathered the duck but, instead of swimming back through the icy river, she stood for a moment on the bank, looking first at me and then at the water and then, without a backward glance, went galloping away out of sight along the far bank. She had remembered that there was a bridge about a quarter of a mile farther on and so was able to deliver the duck without another cold swim. She had not been along that stretch of river for a year or more.

Twice I saw that old dog bring in two grouse in her mouth at the same time. Another of her quaint habits was to use a forepaw to hand off a door if she thought it was going to slam on her as she went through. I have not yet met another dog capable of thinking that one out.

As Zulu was growing old and was unable to produce offspring, I decided to set about looking for her successor. In a local paper there was an advertisement of a litter of mixed colour Labradors which sounded suitable so I went over to see them, only to find that all had been sold bar one yellow dog. Here was a quandary. I was being offered a yellow dog when I wanted a black bitch. Time was of the essence there being not much time in which to train a pup ready for the next shooting season. After a brief study of his pedigree which appeared satisfactory, I decided he would have to do. I had fallen for a pretty face. I should have known better.

Once the pup, which I had decided to call Whisky, had settled down, I began his training. It was a disaster from the first. Not only was he wild and headstrong, he also appeared to be slightly mad. When sent to look for a dummy in long grass or sugar beet, he would go and stand on his head by it, waving his hind legs in the air. Delay followed before he finally brought in the dummy. Too late, a Labrador expert reported that there were far too many show dogs in his ancestry.

When later, hoping for the best, I took Whisky to some of our covert shoots, he regularly disappeared into the next wood to be driven before the beaters were out of the previous one. My long-suffering fellow shooters laughed at my exasperation, occasionally asking if anyone wanted to buy a good dog.

Whisky in fact had some virtues. He was the only dog on our shoot not afraid of the densest bramble thicket and would emerge from it with the bird and with his face streaming with blood from the thorns. He was also a splendid dog in water and could swim like an otter. I seldom lost a bird when I took

119

him flighting duck.

Even so, after two frustrating seasons, I could stand him no longer, and when Biddy Backhouse, my cousin in Sussex, offered him a home, I happily sent him there; apparently he spent most of his days in her local river.

In place of Whisky came Juno, another black bitch, three months old and untrained. She proved a quick learner and soon became a useful performer in the shooting field.

Juno had a long and happy life, during which she produced a litter of black puppies from which I kept the smallest and what appeared to be the brightest of the litter. I called her Tinker and never regretted my choice. She soon made a name for herself by her diligence and skill in finding runners in thick cover such as sugarbeet.

I so well recall an occasion when, in the dusk, she hunted for more than ten minutes in an enormous sugar beet field, up and down the beet rows after a wing-tipped pheasant while we all stood and watched as she finally brought the bird to hand. All were agreed that it would have won her a field trial stake.

On another occasion Tinker achieved a double retrieve, later recorded in the *Field*. Pheasants were being walked up in a rough field in Angus, when she picked up from its form a half-grown brown leveret. As she was bringing it in to me, a neighbouring gun winged a cock pheasant which at once made a dash for the nearest hedge. Tinker saw the fall and still carrying the hare, went in pursuit. In a short time she came back still carrying the hare and the very lively pheasant.

As she is a small dog, with a correspondingly small mouth, all those who observed the episode were amazed that she was able to carry a live hare and a live pheasant all at the same time.

A second instance of her remarkable intelligence was reported to me by two independent witnesses who observed the incident. I had shot a pheasant whch fell in a wood bounded by an oak pale fence. I sent Tinker after it and she was soon seen inside the wood, carrying the dead bird and trying to push her way through the palings. Failing in this, she was then observed to go along the fence, testing each pale with a forefoot until she found one that was loose enough for her to push it aside and come through with the pheasant. Had the episode not been witnessed by two reliable people, I should have doubted the whole story, as being beyond canine intelligence.

I now come to two that must inevitably, I fear be the last of my long line of four-legged companions. In steadfastness and competence in the field they well maintain the standard of their forerunners.

Tinker has gone, game to the last. She left a daughter Jumbi and a grand-daughter Havoc. Very alike in appearance, they differ greatly in temperament. Jumbi, now rising thirteen years, is a placid, immensely loving creature, still competent to do a day's work in the field.

Havoc is the complete extrovert. By one of Stan Harvey's field trial winners, she is a grand worker, quite undaunted on land and water and with a wonderful nose.

She is interested in all that goes on around her and has also become an enthusiastic gardener. She barks fiercely at the wheel of the garden barrow as it trundles round, and delights in sitting alongside anyone working in the flowerbeds, in hope that they will mislay a glove or better still, will throw it for her to retrieve from the shrubbery.

To end this chapter about my dogs I would like to offer some brief comments on choosing a puppy and training it to the gun. I hasten to say that I am in no way an expert, but having trained ten Labradors of my own, all but one of which became useful working dogs, I believe I have some knowledge of the subject. Training one's own shooting companion is a far more satisfying business than sending the dog away to be professionally trained, or buying one ready-trained at a sky high price.

Before agreeing to buy a pup, you should always ask to be allowed to give it one or two little tests first. So too should a home bred litter be individually tested before deciding which is to be kept. These are the tests which I employ. When taking the pup or pups for their first walks — and preferably without their dam — I note carefully those that carry their tails well and that sniff about in hedges and banks as they go along.

They are the individuals that are already interested in using their noses and will probably prove to have the best scenting powers.

I then test for natural retrieving by throwing some small, light object such as a rolled up glove or sock, even an empty matchbox, and take note of which pup most readily picks up the object and, with a little encouragement, brings it back to me. The most promising candidate will soon reveal itself.

Don't fall for a pretty face. Good looks are, of course, desirable, but for a working dog hunting and retrieving capability is all important. Incidentally, knowledgeable shooting men think that the last born of a litter is often the best of all for intelligence and character. Many very good working gun dogs have no pedigree, but most people like their animal to have a good one, particularly if they propose to sell its offspring.

One hears experts say that training a puppy should not start until it is at the very least six months old. I disagree; provided a young dog is sufficiently well grown and is keen to learn, one cannot start it too young, from perhaps ten weeks onwards, when simple basic training can be given for, say, half an hour a day, as long as the pup shows interest. It must not be allowed to get bored by too much 'dummy work'. Also it is most important that a trainee pup spends as much time as possible in the company of its owner/trainer. In that way it develops its intelligence and broadens its mind. This is far better than leaving it shut up in a kennel for long periods every day.

Finally, gun shyness. This can be a very serious problem but is usually curable with care and patience. To get a dog used to the sound of a gun, every day, when the pup has its nose in its dinner bowl, make a few sudden noises like hand clapping, bursting blown-up paper bags or firing caps from a toy pistol. If the pupil seems scared and stops eating, desist at once, or make the noises from further away. In my experience most gun dog puppies very quickly get used to gunshots. Even so, training must be done very gradually; don't hurry things. I continue the process of bursting paper bags near the feeding pup for ten days or so before moving on to the next stage, which is to get someone to fire shots from a 4.10 gun some way away, and out of sight, gradually getting nearer until the pupil can see the gun and will realise that the noise comes from it.

The last stage is to get it used to the much louder noise made by a 12 bore gun. Try taking the dog to a clay pigeon shoot. It can sit in the car at first, some distance away, but gradually can be taken nearer to the noise as it gains confidence.

Above all never, never fire a gun anywhere near a young dog until it shows no fear whatever at the sight and sound of a gun. A puppy that comes from a long line of gun trained ancestors will soon take to it all and become passionately fond of guns and shooting. By frightening it early in life, you can make it permanently gun shy. Don't despair. I have cured two dogs which appeared to be beyond hope in that respect.

Never hurry the training process. Remember you are producing a companion to share your sport for perhaps a quarter of a lifetime. That is not to be lightly undertaken.

10

SUFFOLK DESPOILED

Released back to civilian life in the spring of 1946, I returned to my native Suffolk having been away from home just one month short of six years.

Letters from friends had warned me of some of the changes to expect in our countryside, and I had seen something of them myself during a brief sick leave in the previous July; but the reality was worse than anything I could possibly have imagined. I was absolutely appalled. Wherever I went I found the old familiar landscape had been transformed, so many of its woods and water meadows, its hedges, ponds and marshes which I had known and loved since early childhood, had simply disappeared. New farming practices and the huge new machinery that had evolved during the war years and their aftermath, had brought about changes in the countryside greater and more extreme than anything that had taken place on farms and fields during the previous one hundred years.

Most distressing for me, indeed almost unbelievable, were the changes that had taken place in the immediate vicinity of my home. Much of the once so familiar landscape had disappeared altogether. The four beautiful old meadows that girdled the house and garden on three sides had been ploughed up, their tall hedges and old hedgerow trees uprooted. In springtime they had always brightened our days with their sheets of cowslips, early orchis and lady's smock and in

125

autumn, cows and horses grazed beneath our windows. Saddest of all was the disappearance of the group of great horse chestnut trees that had been such a feature of Maddy's Meadow, among the sweeping branches of which generations of Hartest children had played and generations of courting couples had dallied.

All had gone; the whole of that peaceful rural scene had been swept away and in its place we looked out upon a featureless prairie, a wasteland of stark plough or unrelieved corn crops throughout the year.

At Somerton yet another woeful scene awaited me. The cluster of small fields and meadows which had sheltered the church and churchyard was now one great bare expanse. All its trees and hedges had gone — those lovely centuries old hedges — where every autumn we had picked blackberries and sloes and where, since my earliest days with the gun, I had hunted rabbits and the occasional pheasant. In the valley below, the meadows, with their willow trees and rushy bogs over which the nesting snipe had drummed every spring as far back as I could remember, had been drained and become just another cornfield.

Worse still, the most painful shock of all awaited me, when I made my way towards Lovers Lane, the ancient green lane and cartway which, for centuries had provided a pleasant short cut for Somerton folk down to the Dene Farm and on to Hawkedon village beyond. Lined with old oaks and elm trees, it had been the chief feature of the landscape and of my father's shoot, a regular haunt of pheasants and sometimes of a woodcock or two. Violets, oxlips and purple orchis had brightened its banks and verges in spring, and every year, as long as I had known the old lane, a pair of kestrels had reared their young in a hole in one of the elms. We had always cherished them there, though I had once been allowed to climb up to the nest and bring home in triumph one of the chestnut brown eggs.

To visit that old lane again after six years' absence — during which it had often been in my thoughts — would have given me the greatest pleasure, yet I looked for it in vain. Lovers

126

Lane had simply ceased to exist: the entire lane, its trees and hedges and its dark old pond had been totally erased from the landscape.

In succeeding weeks, as I journeyed about Suffolk, visiting the many places I had known so well in pre-war days, it was evident that the devastation of the landscape had not been confined only to the neighbourhood of my home. In places it was even worse; the centre of the county had suffered particularly, as had the old wild Breckland, much of which, formerly considered unfit for cultivation even during the Great War, was growing crops of barley, rye and sugar beet. Parts of coastal Suffolk, alone, had escaped spoilation by the agricultural juggernaut. There the large estates had managed to preserve some of their natural beauty and with it their wildlife habitat, while playing their full part in food production.

But elsewhere, no matter where I went, it was sadly obvious that during the six years of the war a great part of Suffolk's old rural landscape had been transformed, almost out of recognition.

When I think back to that old pre-war Suffolk, to its chequerboard of small fields sheltered by their great hedges, its slow farming methods, its narrow roads, many of them unmetalled, on which horses and carts and rumbling farm wagons were as often to be seen as cars, or to its deserted beaches on which I often wandered all day long and scarcely met another human soul, I can almost believe I must be thinking of some other part of the world altogether.

Could anyone have forseen, would any naturalist have believed, that within a span of only five decades so much of the landscape, so much of its swarming wildlife, would have disappeared, probably for ever?

Old friends who were farming in Suffolk during the war years, and who usually share my robustly expressed feelings on the slaughter of the countryside, rightly remind me that the increased food production resulting from it was absolutely vital if Britain were not to starve.

Of course, that is fair comment. Britain did not starve, though it was often a close run thing. During the six years of conflict, pressurised by the county's War Agriculture Committee, our farmers turned over to food production part of their land which had never been cultivated before, even in the Great War. By so doing they greatly increased the output of food for the nation. By so doing they also swept away vast expanses of our age old countryside. It was, I suppose, inevitable.

Nevertheless, what distresses countryfolk and naturalists like me has been the ruthless and often unnecessary destruction of so much of the habitat that survived the war — old hedges, green lanes, heath and ponds — at the behest of the European Community's wasteful and spendthrift Common Agricultural Policy (CAP). Its only result has been the creation of vast surpluses of agricultural produce throughout much of Europe, which nobody seems to want and which have proved enormously costly to store.

Over the centuries the Suffolk landscape had undergone many physical changes, some purely local, others, like the Enclosures Acts of the eighteenth century, far reaching and fundamental; but none can have had a greater impact on its rural life, and particularly on its fauna and flora, than the metamorphosis that took place during the Second World War and in the years that followed it.

During the period leading up to the war East Anglian farming went through difficult times. I recall all too clearly how some of Suffolk's best wheat growing land had become derelict, its fields covered with couch grass, brambles and scrub, a haven for partridges and hares and for small birds in numbers undreamed of today, but disastrous for village communities where so many depended on the land for a living. Everywhere farms were for sale and village shopkeepers going out of business. Nobody could wish to see such conditions again.

Yet, looking back, I cannot help thinking that despite their troubles, farmers and their men had a greater feeling for the countryside than is the case today. They were closer to the land in every way and more inclined to protect its environment. They had no wish to grub up hedges and scrubland where birds nested and foxes found harbour, nor to fill in the old field ponds with their populations of fish, newts and dragonflies which had, over the years, given delight to generations of village children as well as to many of their elders. Those who lived on and by the land then had a close affinity with the wild things which they saw almost daily as they went about the fields and woods. They were an integral part of the pattern of the countryside.

What a lot of country lore I learned in my boyhood days from them all; how many interesting facts — as well as interesting fictions — were imparted as I walked and gossiped with my friends the farmers and farm labourers, and still more with the gamekeepers who lived around my home. Some of the farmers hunted and most of them liked a day out with the gun. Ferreting was one of the chief occupations of their men on winter afternoons and many of them enjoyed going out as "brushers" on the big shoots.

The farmworker of those days could turn his hand to almost anything connected with the land and he took real pride in the wellbeing of the farm on which, often, he had worked since boyhood. When he trimmed or laid a hedge he did it with loving care, sparing the saplings of oak and ash, crab apple and elm which he hoped would one day grow into fine trees to shade the stock and break the force of the wind. As he worked with his horse drawn implements he had time to spot the lapwing's nest on a fallow field and to move her eggs away from his roller or harrow and mark the position of any partridges' nests he might discover on a hedgebank in order to show it to his employer or to the estate gamekeeper when he came on his rounds. His successor, the farm mechanic of today, with his roaring combine harvester and clattering hedge trimmer or flail, has little time to notice such things.

Old timers who have spent most of their working lives on arable farms shake their heads at the way they consider the land has been maltreated since the war. 'All the hedges pulled up,' they say; 'white straw after white straw, no stock in the barns, so no muck on the land, nothing but blasted chemicals.'

Pre-war arable farming was very different from what it is today. It was altogether a more leisurely business. Horse ploughs and wooden wagons did not make for speed, and farm work was more evenly spread throughout the year. There was none of the mad scramble which epitomises modern agricultural activities when stubbles are ploughed up, often by night, almost before the last combine has left the field. Little spring corn is now grown and one never sees those red clover fields, once so beloved of partridges and butterflies. Few stubbles now remain unploughed after October.

Today's farming seems to be all rush and roar. It is a highly mechanised, highly specialised and highly capitalised business with no vocational nonense about it. Too many farmers, particularly the young ones look upon their land as little more than a profit producing factory. Anything likely to interfere with the profitable running of that factory must be eliminated, be it bird or beast, hedgerow, tree or pond. The intensive farming now practised produces what farmers call good clean crops, which of course they are, having had anything up to half a dozen different kinds of chemical sprays poured upon them. Scarcely a weed is to be seen in them. They are thick and level and look solid enough to walk upon. They may delight the farmer's eye but the naturalist and lover of the countryside views them very differently. No wild creature can find a home in them.

A year or two ago I was travelling in the great corn lands of Romania. It was an immensely depressing experience. Everywhere we saw enormous fields of wheat, barley and maize which stretched unbroken from horizon to horizon — often at least ten square miles of them — without a tree or bush or building to break the appalling monotony of the landscape. We saw no life of any kind there except the gangs of peasant women hoeing the crops or resting in lethargic groups by the roadside. When, later, I heard a speaker on the BBC radio programme *Farming Today* describe, with apparent awe, how he had just seen in Lincolnshire a wheatfield of over one hundred acres in extent, I could not help wondering whether this could be the shape of things to come, here in East Anglia.

Although it is now forty and more years since the war's end, the same sad tale continues to unfold. Bulldozers still roar across the fields, slicing away still more of the few surviving hedgerows and filling in more of the old ponds.

Our rivers and river valleys have lost much of their beauty and still more of their flora and fauna since the local water boards have taken control of them. Every year their gangs appear to tidy up, trimming down all the bankside herbage, lopping overhanging trees and branches. Periodically they come to scrape and scour the riverbeds until they are reduced to little more than shallow canals, bereft of their once teaming aquatic life. Corn crops and sugar beet now occupy most of the old water meadows where snipe, redshank and wild duck once found homes, and such a variety of wild flowers flourished.

On our Suffolk coast most of the sandlings have disappeared under the plough or beneath bricks and mortar. They once stretched almost without a break from Ipswich to Lowestoft. Just in time a few relic areas have been saved by the RSPB or the Suffolk Wildlife Trust. In the north west only about fifteen per cent of the unique Breckland has been left inviolate. Elsewhere in the county still less common land has escaped the plough or development, a word that now covers such a multitude of ecological horrors. In the spring the countryside stinks of the various chemicals being poured upon the land, the residues of which pollute our rivers and streams, as do the now regular spillages of farm slurry and effluents. Ten thousand fish were killed recently by one such spillage into the River Blackbourne. Many corn crops apparently now need no fewer than six different applications of pesticides between sowing and harvesting.

What becomes of the residue of all those chemicals which the soil must absorb year after year? How is that cocktail affecting, in the long term, the whole ecosystem of our countryside? Does anyone really know? Do chemical residues just disappear between their application one year and use of yet another chemical or chemicals on the same field the following season? Surely not. Some must remain, their properties lingering on.

The experts tell us that some of the chemicals now in regular use break down when in contact with the soil. Yet obviously

131

not all do so. What effect, if any, do those residues have on the land? In any case, should we not be alarmed that farmworkers now have to be safeguarded with masks, goggles and plastic overalls when working with the substances that modern agriculture finds necessary to maintain maximum yields? The potential dangers are obvious. A few years ago a young farmworker living near my home was inadequately protected when using some form of agricultural spray. He became very ill and has had to give up all farm work and go to live in a town.

There have been other cases and must inevitably be more still when potentially harmful insecticides and herbicides are in such widespread use on the land and in fruit orchards. The agrochemist claims that the danger to humans is minimal if chemicals are properly handled: but *are* they always handled and applied with the necessary care?

There are few signs that any safeguards are in regular operation to protect wild creatures living on farmland which must inevitably come in contact with pesticides of greater or lesser toxidity. I am always very chary of exercising myself and my dogs on footpaths and lanes when the crop spraying season is at its height.

Whatever the pros and cons of the matter, it has long been evident — except to those who do not wish to know — that while intensive farming and horticulture on the scale now prevailing may have revolutionised cheap food production, and benefitted the farming industry, it has, at the same time, altered rural life very considerably and often for the worse. It has also brought about an enormous decrease in most of our fauna and flora.

How can it be otherwise? Where can birds now find food and shelter throughout the year and secure nesting places in summer, when our farmland has been stripped bare of so much of its natural cover?

All too much arable farmland consists now of great featureless expanses — they can scarcely be called fields — hedgeless and treeless, blanketted throughout the year beneath acres of corn and sugar beet crops or of stark ploughland. All too little remains of those flowery meadows and green lanes which butterflies need for survival, or of the hedges and hedgebanks which once gave harbour to a huge population of birds, small mammals, insects and wild flowers.

This is sadly depressing for elderly countryfolk like me — and we are getting somewhat thin on the ground — when we look back to the old Suffolk, with its innumerable birds in fields and gardens, its red squirrels and grasshoppers, its glow worms and its myriad butterflies which flew in summer over pasture and roadside. Has that delightful unkempt, unshaven, totally rustic landscape gone for ever?

As long ago as 1978 I wrote in the Introduction to my *Birds of Suffolk*: 'Modern agricultural practices are harmful to a greater or lesser extent to most wild creatures and here in Suffolk we have already lost much of our wildlife'. A recent pamphlet *Lowland Farming*, published by the Nature Conservancy Council, underlines the position in unequivocal terms: 'Farmland under crops,' it says, 'supports little wildlife. Few animals and plants can survive regular ploughing and spraying with chemicals'.

That sad fact becomes more obvious with the passing years. In general, modern man's activities in the countryside are, by their very nature, harmful to some extent and often catastrophically so, to much of our wildlife and its habitat. This is particularly so when they are carried to extremes as has happened, and is still happening, in Britain's corn growing regions. Suffolk is said to be among the worst affected; from personal observation I should say that parts of Cambridgeshire and Northamptonshire are equally as bad.

Wild creatures face many other perils besides those that arise from intensive farming. The steadily increasing volume of traffic on our country roads must be responsible for the deaths of enormous numbers of birds and beasts. The evidence is there for all to see; the corpses of birds, large and small, hares, hedgehogs, frogs and toads — even badgers and deer — lie on or beside the carriageway, but the speeding motorist sees little of them and apparently cares less. Only last summer I was driving behind a woman whose car struck a young turtle dove as it flew across the road. Without so much as a backward glance, the driver continued on her way leaving the bird floundering on the road amid a cloud of feathers. She must have known what she had done and could so easily have pulled to the side for a few moments to see whether the bird was still alive. Instead she drove on.

I stopped, as I always do under such circumstances, gathered up the bird which still showed signs of life, and took it home with me. It recovered after a few days with food and water in my greenhouse. Many such casualties prove to be only stunned and will recover if moved to safety in time.

Another less obvious danger to birdlife arises from the miles of power lines and other wires which now festoon the landscape. They are a constant threat to flocks of migrant birds flying after dark or in foggy weather. Whenever I have walked along beneath a line of pylons crossing open country I have been saddened by the number of bird casualties, mainly of larger species like waders, geese, ducks and grouse, lying beneath the wires. In Scotland I once counted sixteen redwings killed by flying at night into a short stretch of telephone wires. A year or two ago I also saw nearly a score of Canada geese lying dead under a line of pylons at Lackford.

Of all the threats and hazards to which our wildlife is exposed, by far the most serious is the destruction of natural habitat. Year by year more of the countryside is being swallowed up by bricks and mortar, or is sliced away to make room for new roads or village bypasses.

Unquestionably, a great deal of the responsibility for the loss of so much of Britain's landscape, and the huge decrease in its flora and fauna, must lie with past governments and their legislation — or lack of it. In the years that followed the end of the Great War, a number of Acts of Parliament were passed, designed to give protection in some form to Britain's wild birds. Little or nothing was done to protect butterflies and wild flowers.

During that time such bird protection laws as existed were largely ineffectual; indeed, they were often ignored altogether. Only a comparatively small number of dedicated bird lovers took them seriously and tried to ensure that they were enforced. The general public was indifferent. There was little encouragement for it to be otherwise. Most country boys collected birds' eggs, as did many adults, some of them in a very big way.

Even after the last war few bird species were protected except during the breeding season between March and July. This was adequate enough at that time when most of our birdlife was abundant — even very abundant — and protection was needed only for a few birds of prey which were visibly declining in numbers. It seems never to have occurred to our legislators that they should give protection to important wildlife habitat, a word seldom heard in those days. Why should it? There was no obvious threat then to the countryside and its physical features.

For generations trees were cut down only when necessary, if they became dangerous, or were needed to provide building material or firewood. Landlords coppiced their woodlands every seven years or so, and replanted them once in a generation. Farmers cleaned out their ponds and ditches as and when required. Old meadowland was managed in a regular annual cycle, being harrowed in spring, cut for hay in summer, then grazed by stock till winter set in. This resulted in a wonderfully balanced ecosystem for plant and insect life which also benefitted a number of avian species, particularly skylarks and English partridges.

Marshes, heathlands, water meadows and miles of hedges flourished, all part of a landscape unchanged for centuries, and likely to remain so. Wholesale hedgerow removal, the felling and grubbing of old woodland, as well as the draining of ponds and marshes were ecological horrors yet to come.

But come they did, and with a vengeance. During the past half century we have seen — and it has been almost entirely the result of habitat destruction — a quite enormous decrease in much of our wildlife, even amongst the once common species, while a number of butterflies and still more wild flowers, have disappeared altogether.

For years now naturalists and conservationists have been striving to convince the National Farmers' Union (NFU) and all those involved in agriculture, as well as the general public and, most important of all, our legislators, that rapid and drastic action is needed if our flora and fauna and its all important habitat, is not to be lost for ever.

For my part, I have been trying for more than forty years now, as a WEA tutor, or when lecturing on wildlife matters to Women's Institutes, bird and field Clubs, at Rotary lunches and the like, to impress on those who do not already realise it, how vital is the need for all of us to preserve and protect every possible piece of what still remains of our countryside. Every small copse and rough pasture, every pond and blackthorn thicket is important as the habitation of so many wild creatures great and small, and all need to be preserved. Mankind's activities threaten them all.

Until recently our efforts were largely in vain. Successive governments showed little interest and for far too long it was left to private bodies like the Royal Society of Protection of Birds and the Royal Society of Nature Conservation to take steps to preserve valuable wilderness areas.

One county only — Norfolk — had the foresight and enterprise to acquire such areas while there was still time. The establishment of county wildlife trusts which now cover most of lowland Britain, had to wait until well after the last war. Only within recent years has the protection of the countryside and its wild creatures become of interest to our legislators. Formerly there was thought to be few votes in it but now, suddenly, the environment has become important, green is good and politicians are at last prepared to take action.

In 1981 Parliament passed the Wildlife and Countryside Act, a measure wide ranging in its aims and objectives provided — but only provided — they are strictly and properly implemented. Up to now this has not always been the case. Its conditions are all too easily ignored or circumvented by industrialists, local councils, private individuals and even, in some cases, by government ministers.

Recent Chancellors of the Exchequer, who should have been better advised, have even seen fit to provide public funds enabling companies and individuals to obtain considerable tax advantages by planting large tracts of Britain's rapidly dwindling heather moors with conifers and this in face of the strongest possible opposition from the Nature Conservancy Council and other conservation bodies. Afforestation of a large part of the Flo country of Sutherland and Caithness, a unique wilderness area with a unique breeding bird population, has been a particularly disgraceful example of misguided policy. There have been many other such instances in Scotland and Wales.

A survey by the Countryside Commission and the Department of the Environment has revealed that since 1945 more than two hundred thousand miles of British hedgerows have been grubbed up. Five thousand miles of hedges lost each year seems a heavy price to pay for a little extra land on which to produce more unwanted crops to add to the already huge surplus in store.

Here in Suffolk the result is plain to see in the great featureless expanses of arable land devoted solely to corn and sugar beet. Was it all necessary and inevitable, or was it just another example of the CAP's insensate folly?

Equally serious losses have taken place in Britain's old meadowland where barely one per cent of that which existed in 1945 survives today. In Suffolk, according to the Suffolk Wildlife Trust, more than eighty-five per cent of its Breckland and sandlings have been lost to forestry or agriculture. More than half the marshes have also disappeared. As a result, the natural pattern of our countryside has been changed almost beyond recognition.

Those who only know the Suffolk of today may well not realise the extent to which its landscape has been transformed over the past fifty years. They may consider it to be an attractive, even beautiful county, as of course it is — in places.

Pockets of countryside are still to be found, even quite considerable areas of mixed farmland and woods which, outwardly at least, seem to have changed very little since pre-war days. While these scattered, often fragmented areas still support a modicum of their once abundant flora and fauna, by contrast, far too much has been reduced to a featureless, monocultural wasteland which has recently been described as being 'about as aesthetically pleasing as a slagheap'.

11

WITH DOG AND GUN —
AT HOME AND OVERSEAS

Those of us who shoot wild game in Britain nowadays — and I use the word game in its broadest sense — can be conveniently classified under three main headings: wildfowlers, roughshooters and those who take part only in organised driven shoots. There are also, of course, a considerable number of pigeon shooters.

The characteristic of the first two, and the one that particularly distinguishes them from the third, is the fact that they are largely self sufficient, depending for the success of their sport only on themselves, their dogs, their knowledge of fieldcraft and the habits and likely behaviour of their quarry. Most of them are countrymen and good naturalists, as indeed they need to be. Furthermore the birds and beasts which provide them with their sport are generally wild in every sense of the word.

The third group, probably the least numerous, do most of their shooting as members of organised parties where the game is driven to them by a line of beaters, aided by what are known as stops and pickers-up, the latter gathering any game that falls dead or wounded behind the guns.

Much — perhaps most — of the game which makes up the bag at such driven shoots is likely to have been hand reared, hatched in incubators or under broody hens, and protected from predators until fully grown and ready to face the free life — and the guns: in general their sporting qualities are not to be compared with those of truly wild birds.

Wildfowlers and roughshooters have much in common and many of them combine the two roles,but both tend to be somewhat contemptuous — or is it a little envious? — of those who have their game driven to them. They assert that shooting driven birds is too easy. This of course, is a fallacy since most driven birds, having flown some distance before they reach the guns, are flying considerably faster and so present a more testing shot than those that rise in front of a walking gun. I can speak in full knowledge of the subject for I have long worn all three hats. Throughout my shooting career, which now spans close on sixty-five years, I have taken an active part in almost all forms of shooting from ferreting rabbits along Suffolk hedgerows, to the more exciting experience of pursuing wild boars in great French forests and Tunisian maquis. Except on days when my personal performance with the gun has fallen far below par, I have enjoyed to the full every aspect of them all. Furthermore, I have — on and off — run shoots for the benefit of others as well as myself since I was seventeen years old, and can also claim to have had considerable practical experience as an amateur gamekeeper.

I have also done a great deal of roughshooting or, as it is generally called, walking up, most of it in East Anglia and Scotland, with a certain amount elsewhere in Britain and, both before and during the last war, in foreign lands.

Like most country boys of my generation, my shooting career began with rabbits — rabbits sitting and rabbits running. From them I progressed to the partridge and at the age of thirteen duly bagged my first in a clover field at my former family home at Somerton.

In the Suffolk of my youth — those two decades that led up to the Second World War, the English partridge was the dominant bird, far more common than the wild pheasant. Our small fields with their thick hedges, the farming methods and the cover crops then grown — turnips and mangolds, red clover, lucerne and potatoes — with stubbles left unploughed until well into the new year, were just what the partridge needed to prosper and prosper it did.

On most arable farms of about one hundred acres or so, which was about the average acreage then, five or six coveys of English partridges with one or two good lots of redlegs, were generally to be found after a reasonable breeding season. On the well keepered estates of five hundred acres and upwards, of which there were a good number in those days, partridges were usually driven, with bags from fifty brace upwards.

Wild pheasants were far less plentiful then and on only a comparatively few shoots were hand reared birds put down in any number. A bag of two hundred pheasants was then considered to be quite sufficient for a day's sport, as they still should be.

In the 1930s, when partridge stocks allowed, driving took place right through to the end of January and this made no obvious difference to the bags the following season.

For both partridge driving and cover shoots for pheasants, the number of guns in those days was usually limited to six or seven; greater numbers were frowned upon as 'not done'. Today one often sees parties of nine or more guns, which is undesirable in every way.

My father, who used to shoot two or three days a week in winter throughout much of his life, told me that on some of the big estates in Suffolk and Norfolk a method of driving partridges known as 'cornering' was often used during the 1914-18 war. Four guns only took part, standing two on each side of the junction of two tall hedges and the beaters drove to that point. When snow lay for long periods on the fields, he and his friends used to wear white nightshirts over their clothes for camouflage.

My old friend Fletcher le Fleming, who lived for many years at Thurlow, is the only person I have ever met who has seen 'kiting' practiced. In years past, when partridges had become wild and some birds were needed for the table, one or two guns would go out with the gamekeeper, who flew a kite, designed to look like a hawk, over the fields. This made the coveys sit

141

tight. Fletcher had taken part in such proceedings himself.

Much as I enjoy driven shoots, particularly when grouse and genuine wild partridges are the quarry, I find that walking up in the company of a few like minded friends, and a beater or two, gives me more pleasure than the biggest driven day at pheasants. There are so many incidentals in such a day. It usually takes place in attractive, varied country: guns and beaters can chaff each other, reminiscing as they go; interesting birds or beasts may show up — while I never tire of watching spaniels and retrievers at work. Above all, the bag is often a very mixed one in which woodcock, snipe and a duck or two may figure, besides the more usual game and, north of the Borders, a wild goose, golden plover or blackcock may also add variety to the bag.

Wildfowling is also a form of roughshooting, indeed often very rough, and from early youth until advancing years and physical infirmity put a stop to it, I was a passionate devotee, making regular forays after duck and geese from Lincolnshire to the Solway and to the Western Isles of Scotland.

A hazardous sport at the best of times, wildfowling is indulged in only by hardy types, and every year we hear of fowlers who lose their lives when caught out on the mudflats by a rising tide or by some other hazard. Twice I have been in some peril when indulging in it. The first occasion was when my labrador Trigger went through the ice on the River Bure when I was flighting in icy conditions with Robin Harrison. I had already gone in above my waist in an effort to reach her when, luckily, she managed to beak her way ashore.

To have to listen to the sounds of a drowning dog, or still worse I suppose, to watch one doing so, must be a truly awful experience. Years ago, when I first went fowling along the Norfolk shore, an old Blakeney gunner gave me a blood chilling account of how he and others with him had to stand impotently by, one dark winter's night, while they listened to the cries and gradually fading whimpers of one of their dogs which had gone through the ice on a Norfolk mere while trying to retrieve a dead duck. More than one fowler has died when going to the aid of a much loved dog in difficulties.

My second near shave was on the Friskney Shore in Lincolnshire when I was trying to get up to a pack of Brent geese by stalking them under cover of a low mudbank by the deep water channel. They were not then a protected species. I was wearing thigh boots and was almost within shot of my quarry when my feet slipped on the sloping sides and in I went up to my armpits. Only wildfowlers will know what it feels like to be in such a situation, with boots full of icy water dragging one down, and no foothold in the glutinous mud below. I remember how desparately I threw the gun ashore, and myself face downwards, while I clawed with both hands at the greasy mudbank. It seemed an age before I managed to haul myself on to firm ground to face the long tramp in dripping clothes across a mile or more of saltings to the haven of my car.

There were, though, other happier and more successful forays alone or with a friend along the tideline or on inland marshes and bogs. Nights after widgeon under the moon in Lincolnshire with John Darley and that wicked old genius Mackenzie Thorpe, and on the Solway Firth where I shot my first right-and-left at graylags after a long stalk waist deep down an icy burn, as the great birds clawed their way seawards in half a gale.

Thinking back to that first fowling trip to the Solway brings to mind a little episode connected with the train journey up there.

It was in 1947 and, with petrol still rationed, I had decided to travel up by train to my destination near Annan. I had my old dog Trigger with me. The day proved foggy and my train got later and later until finally it gave up the struggle at Carlisle where I sought shelter at the Station Hotel — it being past eight and quite dark. I asked for a bed and a meal. A bed certainly, said the young receptionist, but sadly there was no chance of a meal; the restaurant was closed and the cook had gone home. There could be nothing until breakfast next morning.

A harrowing account of my long, cold journey with nothing to eat since lunch, did nothing to soften the maiden's heart, but when I asked for some scraps for the dog, reaction was swift and positive. An enormous bowl of bits and pieces appeared and with it Trigger and I retired upstairs to my bedroom where we duly shared, and mutually enjoyed, the mixed delicacies.

Although, in the army, we often talked of a "dog's breakfast" when military matters went awry — and one of my cousins once ate his dog's dinner in mistake for the one his wife had left for him in the oven — those Carlisle scraps have long lingered in my memory as what must surely be one of the most unorthodox of wildfowlers' suppers. I can think of one other; bits of graylag goose, cooked on makeshift spits over a driftwood fire one night in a ruined Hebridean chapel, in which four of us and three dogs were marooned without any other food for twenty-four hours.

I returned home from that first foray to the Solway with my graylags and a number of wigeon in a bag. I also returned with an acute attack of what is known as goose fever. All wildfowlers worthy of the name — be they young or not so young — tend to catch goose fever at some stage of their shooting career. This complaint will send them sallying out with the gun, often in the foulest weather imaginable, to some of the remotest parts of our islands, where the great skeins of grey geese are flying and their glorious wild clamour fills the sky and stirs the human spirit.

I had the fever very seriously for two decades or more. It led me to spend several of my annual shooting holidays in the Western Isles of Scotland. Islay, one of the Inner Hebrides, was my favourite. It is a glorious island for the gunner naturalist, with an abundance of game and wildfowl besides interesting birds such as eagles and choughs. It is also well known for its large winter population of barnacle geese, graylags and Greenland white-fronted geese, a handsome dark race with a wonderful musical cry. I hoped to wing-tip one or two of the latter to add to my collection at Hartest. Within a day or two of my arrival I was lucky enough to fall in with a friendly ex-naval farmer who did not shoot but kindly gave me the run of his heathery, boggy domain on which almost every kind of game and wildfowl was to be found.

I soon discovered where one of the regular flight lines of the white-fronts crossed his land and there one evening a small gaggle came within shot. I saw the leader stagger as I fired and slide away down into the grey dusk. I had Trigger with me and sent her off after it. Time passed — five minutes — ten minutes — but with no sign of dog or goose, so I set off walking down the line I thought they had taken and there, presently, my torch revealed a tableau — Trigger standing motionless, tail wagging softly and opposite her the goose, also standing its ground, with one wing raised like a boxer. The bird seemed unharmed bar a broken wing tip, so I gathered it up in my coat and took it back to the pub where I was staying. There, in an empty hen run where it was safe from prowlers, it settled down quite happily and within two days was eating soaked bread and dog biscuits. Its subsequent history is related in Chapter Seven.

For several years, Bob, John and Kathleen Darley, old Suffolk friends, joined me either on Islay or North Uist or at Kilberry on the Mull of Kintyre, where we enjoyed some supremely happy weeks after geese and duck, grouse and woodcock. On one well remembered occasion, Kathleen succeeded in driving a pack of black grouse over us, out of which I duly took my first blackcock.

The purist may say that the only true wildfowling is to be had within sight and smell of the tides. Be that as it may, I rate what is known as the evening flight for duck, whether it is by tidal creek or sea wall, by loch side or inland flight pond, as the absolute acme of wildfowling and even, perhaps, of all forms of shooting.

I must have stood the flight many scores of times in different parts of Britain, as well as in France and North Africa, and frequently without firing a shot, yet always the enjoyment and interest, indeed the excitement of it all, remains undimmed.

Let me set the scene for you. It is twilight on a grey October evening and you are standing, let us suppose, by some expanse of reed, mud and water; probably it is a secluded marsh pool or flooded pasture or flight pond, to which you expect, or at

145

least fondly hope, that mallard and teal will presently come flighting in while it is still light enough to see them. A preliminary reconnaisance has shown you, by scattered feathers and droppings, that the site is being visited regularly by duck.

You are all alone in the silent countryside, except for your regular shooting companion, the dog that sits watchfully beside you. The light is fading fast. You stand alert, all senses tensed for sight and sound, your eyes ranging across the after glow where visibility is still reasonable, to the deepening grey dusk against which shadowy flying shapes will be hard to see. You cast fleeting glances at the dog; its pricked ears, like radar, will hear the sound of wings long before you can.

The daylight has almost gone; it is the magic hour. All around you are the night sounds, the 'frau frau' of wings, the voices of waders and moorhens, the rustles and squeaks in the herbage.

Suddenly, with a hiss of wings and a soft plop, a lone teal drops down on to the water, too quick and too low for a shot, but the flight has begun. A moment later three gray shapes — they are mallard — come corkscrewing down, with a sound like tearing paper. You drop one but miss with your second barrel as the others flare up and away. If you are lucky during the next half hour or so you will have perhaps a dozen other chances and your dog will have plenty of work to do until the shooting light has gone and you can both go home to tea.

In a lifetime's sport with the shotgun, during which I have been lucky enough to be able to enter in my game book one or more examples of every sporting bird, as well as most of the wildfowl normally found in Britain, I have also had opportunities to do a certain amount of small game shooting in foreign lands. In the 1930s, in part of eastern Poland, later seized by the Russians, two of us had several interesting days walking up grey partridges in enormous fields of tall barley stubble and blue lupins. The many small lakes there also held mallard, teal, garganey and pochard and there I saw and shot my first great snipe. Some years later, during the fighting in Italy, I took a right-and-left at great snipe flushed from the edge of a flooded rice field. That cannot be a unique achievemment but I have never yet met anyone else who can claim to have done it.

While serving in Tunisia in 1943, I managed to keep our regimental mess supplied, when opportunity offered itself, with some of the local Barbary partridges, handsome creatures rather larger than our own redlegs, with chestnut and white collars. Later, when heavy rains flooded large stretches of farmland, great numbers of duck and geese came pouring in from Europe but a sad lack of cartridges precluded more than an occasional foray after them.

Tunisia in winter had much besides ducks to offer in the way of sport. Wild boars were plentiful in the forest and maquis covered foothills and the local French farmers were always ready to organise drives for our benefit. I took part in a number of them. Most of us used 12-bore shotguns loaded with heavy shot or what is known as paradox, a heavy slug rifled internally for use in a smooth-bore gun. Those who had no shotguns used the .303 service rifles. Some Australian airmen who were encamped near us liked to fire incendiary bullets from their rifles but, so far as I could see, with singularly little success; the bullets tended to set the dry scrub alight behind the galloping pigs.

Before one such shoot we had all been invited to a farmhouse for drinks. Enormous glasses of arak were handed round. I always think arak a respulsive drink and was wondering how to dispose of mine without offending our hosts. Looking round the very crowded room, I observed that the French farmer standing next to me had his gun slung muzzle upwards from his shoulder in the usual continental fashion. This opportunity was too good to miss: while its owner's attention was directed elsewhere, I, to my shame, softely tipped the contents of my glass down his gun barrels and moved discreetly away. I was able to enjoy the tumult that arose when the gun was reversed and a stream of arak gushed out on to the floor.

One pig was shot that day and pieces of it were put to grill over an open fire, while we all stood around discussing the sport. I recall watching with admiration how Brigadier Noel Tetley duly received from an Arab's dirty fingers and ate, without so much as a grimace, a portion of liver burnt to a cinder outside but still quite raw within. It was the act of a true gentleman.

I had a number of other interesting outings after wild boars in the Tunisian hills, including one night spent sitting up with the local garde champetre — a kind of gamekeeper — in a vineyard, in the hope of ambushing raiding pigs. Although we both heard loud champings and grunts, and saw grey figures in the distance, neither of us got a shot. Later, another farmer arranged a pig drive for a companion and me. The three of us were positioned in a narrow wadi in the thickly wooded hills above the farmhouse while the farmers' Arab labourers drove a considerable area towards us. After a time loud shouts warned us that the game was on the move and soon a large sow and her litter of half grown piglets came charging down the wadi. The farmer fired at the sow and broke a foreleg but, even so, she came galloping furiously at him with her mouth open, until he killed her with a second shot.

The other gun and I each brought down one of the piglets which provided the mess with a delicious meal as a change from army rations.

For a time my regiment formed part of the allied front line before Tunis. When military chores allowed I liked to take an evening stroll with shotgun and binoculars in search of a brace or two of partridges for the mess, or some interesting specimen for the Mammal Room at the Natural History Museum in London, whence my old friend R I Pocock, was regularly urging me to send home small mammals for study.

One evening I shot a partridge which fell into a small wadi. As it hit the ground I was astonished to see a large wild cat bounce out of the bushes, sieze my partridge in its mouth and dive back into cover. A shower of stones soon put the cat on the move again and, with a second shot, into the bag. Suitably skinned and treated, the cat duly reached the Mammal Room where it was welcomed as the first that they had seen from that part of Africa. It resembled, I think, one from Sardinia.

Subsequently, I was able to send the museum skins of a large jackal, a water mongoose, civets, gundis, mice, bats and other

148

lesser but interesting fry.

In Italy, to which we moved in due course, I was invited to take part in a number of other singularly unproductive boar drives. One, organised by a titled landowner, was memorable not for the size of the bag, which consisted of one rabbit, but for a quite superb alfresco lunch served by flunkies in livery at tables set out in the sunshine, and laden with every possible kind of cold meats and wine. The shoot lasted a couple of hours, the lunch about four! Everyone went home happy.

I was fortunate to end my war service in Paris where soon I became acquainted with a number of French landowners who invited me to some splendid shoots, including one two day affair after wild boar. It took place in the Soloigne, a vast area of heath and forest in which we saw not a living soul all day except for the guns and beaters. I was given into the charge of the local miller, a great authority. Small shaggy hounds called griffons were used to rouse the pigs, and the movements of the hounds and game were punctuated by calls on hunting horns. My mentor would listen carefully to the music and announce that they had found, or they had run to the left, or were coming towards us.

The rides were very wide and besides an occasional pig we saw a number of red and roe deer galloping across them. I was surprised that some of the red deer hinds were being shot and butchered on the spot. Before long my mentor whispered 'there, there' and pointed into the dark forest ahead. The next moment a number of grey shapes, with big bat ears, came galloping towards us through the trees. I fired at a large beast as it dodged round the tree trunks and gave it a second barrel before it disappeared into the gloom. I feared that I had missed, but the miller said 'Non, non, vous avez le tirer' and there, a little way inside the wood, we later found the great hairy beast laying dead. It proved to be one of the biggest pigs shot in the hunt and weighed, if I recall correctly, 180 lb. I was duly presented with a haunch to take home and very delicious it proved to be. The dried foot hangs in the hall here as a reminder of a most interesting and exciting experience.

150

12

WHAT OF THE FUTURE

Has the devastation of so much of our Suffolk landscape been halted at last? Can we hope that the decline in the number of its birds and butterflies has been checked if not reversed? Are the signs and portents fabourable? I suppose that in theory at least we can say that they are, but in practice ...?

Certainly the most encouraging sign of change for the better has been the remarkable increase in concern for the protection and wellbeing of the countryside and its wild inhabitants that has become manifest during the past two decades, among town and country folk alike.

More people are reading and learning about birds and beasts, from books and magazines; still more are watching the excellent programmes on different aspects of wild nature that are shown almost daily on our television screens. Most important of all has been the upsurge in the numbers of those now joining conservation societies and trusts.

To cite an example here in Suffolk: in 1961 the late Lord Cranbrook, a dedicated naturalist and conservationist, called together a number of local naturalists with the object of forming a body to be known as The Suffolk Trust for Nature Conservation. During the next fifteen years or so it was only with difficulty that a total membership of some 5,000 enthusiasts was achieved. The wildlife bandwagon had not then begun to roll.

151

Yet by 1992 — and then known as The Suffolk Wildlife Trust — its membership, under very active and enterprising leadership, had risen to nearly 13,000. It continues to add by gift, purchase, or agreement with individual landowners, more pieces of our countryside in which important habitat areas and rare or threatened species can be safeguarded. The trust now has the highest membership of any in Britain. Even so, there is still an immense amount to be done before every piece of worthwhile wild habitat is protected.

As things are now, one would need to be clairvoyant to foretell the future of our countryside during the next twenty or even the next ten years. Human activities and operations which cannot even be guessed at now may well be needed to sustain Britain's steadily growing population and provide it with the services and recreations it seems likely to demand. We shall need more water, more electricity, indeed more of everything. Changes are inevitable and likely to be considerable and far reaching, involving, for better or worse, our countryside and its denizens.

Would it be over optimistic to hope that the future of our countryside will still depend largely, as it has in the past, on the prosperity of the farming industry? Who can say? Prospects certainly do not look propitious. Who can be sure where British agriculture is heading? Will small farms become uneconomic and disappear altogether, or will they become mere hobby farms of small acreage on which those seeking a peaceful, rural lifestyle can keep a pony or two, rear a few geese and fowls and grow fruit and vegetables for themselves and their neighbours?

Alternatively, will intensive farming become still more intensive rather than less so, as arable farmers seek to compensate for falling corn prices by yet more production? If, on the other hand they seek to diversify in other directions by experimenting with strange crops or novel land uses, how will those new enterprises affect wildlife? Will a new golf course prove more beneficial to birds and butterflies than for instance, a fourty acre barley field? Almost certainly it will. I recall how, in the 1930s, the golf course at Flempton supported a very varied flora and fauna. Crossbills nested every year in the fir trees surrounding the clubhouse and mallard, gadwall, teal and snipe found sanctuary within its boundaries.

Will our Government's new-found enthusiasm for all that is green prove resolute enough to withstand adverse pressures which, from past experience, are likely to be exerted by big business, urban and rural councils and unsympathetic bodies and individuals? Only time will show. Its track record to date can scarcely be called reassuring.

If, however, agriculture continues to languish in the doldrums to the extent that seems probable as I write, still more changes are likely to take place in the countryside, affecting human beings and wildlife. Let us hope they will be beneficial for all.

In fact, there are already signs that things are beginning to change for the better. Real gleams of light are to be discerned amid the environmental gloom. The first and probably the most important manifestation of that change has been the quite astonishing upsurge that has taken place in post war Britain in the number of people who now enjoy watching and studying wildlife. Now that people have more mobility and leisure time, watching wild birds and beasts, and studying wild flowers, is proving a wonderful antidote to the stress and strain of modern life. To be a bird watcher or a bat watcher is no longer considered a sign of dottiness or eccentricity, as it was in my youth.

Suffolk's present-day ornithological scene is totally unlike that of the 1930s. There were no wildlife reserves then, nor in general, was much interest shown in birds and butterflies. In those days there were probably fewer than a score of individuals in the whole of Suffolk who would have described bird watching as one of their chief interests. Few kept records of what they saw or passed information on to others.

The Suffolk Naturalists Society was not formed until 1929 nor were there any *Suffolk Bird Reports* until the first appeared in 1950. Ticehurst's *History* was only published in 1932. There was no grapevine for the wide exchange of information. In

West Suffolk I knew of no more than a handful of individuals who would have described themselves as naturalists, let alone as bird watchers. I never saw any of them carrying binoculars. Large areas of the county were *terra incognita*, so far as most of our wildlife was concerned.

Today, by contrast, there are now probably considerably more than one hundred individuals in Suffolk who are interested in and knowledgable about some aspect of its flora or fauna. Where birds are concerned, few rare or unusual species can now pass through the county without being seen, identified and reported by someone. This is, of course liable to produce a somewhat unbalanced picture when we try to compare the present day status of any species with that prevailing in the period between the two wars.

Later I hope to put on record what I remember of Suffolk's varied and abundant wildlife in pre-1940 days. I have my bird diaries dating from 1927 to assist me.

The second and equally important sign of greater concern for the welfare of our countryside and its wildlife has been the increasing number of farming families in Suffolk who have set about reversing the loss of wildlife and restoring its habitat.

Leading pioneers in this crusade have been brothers John and Peter Wilson of Ixworth Thorpe. They began by landscaping and generally improving, for the benefit of wetland species, a number of flooded gravel pits on their home farm. Besides creating several islands in those pits they have levelled the verges to provide stretches of mud and shingle attractive to waders and ducks. As a result, great-crested grebes, dabchicks and several species of ducks, as well as Egyptian geese and little ringed plovers, now stay to breed regularly where formerly only a few birds were likely to remain for an hour or two.

The Wilsons have shown the way to others by using minimal sprays on their corn headlands, as well as limiting the use of pesticides on their land generally. They have built observation hides alongside their ponds, from which visitors can watch the birdlife, and have laid out an interesting nature trail. Otters have been successfully reintroduced on their local river. Their highly successful enterprise attracts many visitors every year and has earned the brothers a considerable number of well deserved awards.

Another farmer, naturalist and conservationist John Digby of Sycamore Farm, Swilland, who for many years made the maintenance of hedgerows and ponds his chief farming priority, has now set aside his entire farm for the protection of wildlife. During a recent visit there I saw more butterflies in one hour than I had seen anywhere else in Suffolk, in any morning, for many years.

The example set by these pioneers is now being followed by more landowners who have realised what can be done with imagination and skill and have discovered, perhaps for the first time, what pleasure is to be had by attracting birds, butterflies and other wild creatures to return and re-colonise suitable wild habitat.

Furthermore, there are a number of independent organisations, such as the Farming and Wildlife Group (FWAG), which advise landowners on how to improve existing habitat or to create new sanctuaries for wildlife on their land.

Prominent among such enterprises in Suffolk has been an extensive survey inspired by the National Farmers Union and carried out by a number of farmers in a group of twenty-eight villages centred on Stanton. Those taking part in what has been called the 'Stanton Survey' have researched and documented historical details of their countryside and its past and present habitat, including hedges removed and hedges now being replanted.

They are actively encouraging others to show interest in the maintenance of and, where possible, the re-establishment of the most important wild featurs of the countryside, lost during the past half century.

The restoration of farmland to something approaching its immensely varied physical appearance in 1939 is, to my mind, the most important of all the many tasks now facing those concerned with wildlife preservation in Suffolk.

For a start we need a sympathetic and steadfast government and not one which puts forward proposals for the betterment of the countryside and then backtracks the moment it receives criticism of the plans. This has happened all too often of recent years, where preservation of, in particular, our hedgerows has been concerned.

Most naturalists will probably agree that until many more hedges and hedgerow trees, shelter belts, copses and ponds are restored to our arable farms, there is little prospect that such birds as skylarks and red linnets, yellowhammers and chaffinches, as well as stock doves and little owls, will ever be seen again on farmland in anything like their pre-war abundance. They were among the birds that, in the 1920s and 1930s helped to make up at least half of the entire biomass of Suffolk's wild birds.

It would be quite unrealistic to expect that the intensive farmer, with his huge and expensive machinery, and his fields of a hundred acres or more, will be able or willing to revert to farming fields of much smaller acreage, nor will he take kindly to being asked to put back hedges to protect his new small fields. Therein lies the crunch: is production of cereal crops, for which there is little or no demand, to continue on our farms subsidised by the taxpayer, at the expense of landscape and wildlife, which an increasing number of people — taxpayers themselves — wish to see restored and protected?

Conservationists' hopes were raised recently when the government announced a plan to protect existing hedgerows, to be called the Hedgerow Notification Scheme. Unfortunately, pressure from landowners swiftly put a stop to the proposal and, later still, a Private Members' Bill introduced with the same protective object was 'talked out' by a handful of obstructive MPs.

In the meantime the importance of hedgerow protection has been strongly underlined by a survey from the Institute of Terrestial Ecology, which showed that in the six years between 1984 and 1990, more than 64,000 miles of hedges had been uprooted or otherwise destroyed.

Fortunately, however, protection of hedgerows and other landscape features has been made easier and less costly for landowners as a result of the quite considerable number of financial aids administered by the Ministry of Agriculture, and now available to those wishing to protect suitable habitat areas on their land. The first and, perhaps, the most valuable, is to protect what are to be known a Environmentally Sensitive Areas — such as the Broads, Suffolk river valleys and Breckland; and high time too in the case of Breckland. So much of that ecologically unique region has been ruined by unwise and unnecessary forestry over the last seventy years, with similar damage done to the habitat of indigenous plants and birds by wartime farming on the old Breck.

What are known as Landscape Conservation Grants are also available now to encourage the restoration of old hedges, hay meadows and ponds. Encouraged by FWAG, some sixty miles of new hedgerows have been planted. This is a start.

Until the last war, Suffolk was a land of ponds; almost every meadow and many of its arable fields contained one or more of them. The meadow ponds were valuable watering places for cattle and horses throughout the year; others had no regular use but were, in their own right, wonderfully secluded oases where fish, frogs, dragonflies and moorhens lived out their lives and mallard ducks came to nest and occasional kingfishers to fish. They lay almost undisturbed throughout the year, except when the fields were being cultivated or when birds' nesting small boys found their way to them in spring.

Then came the war and most of the ponds on arable land were filled in and cultivated, or were used as dumps for farm rubbish — eyesores filled with old bedsteads and mattresses, tangles of wire and wire netting and old weedkiller tins. The Suffolk Wildlife Trust is now cleaning out and restoring many of such ponds to become, once again, valuable habitat for wildlife.

There is yet one more agricultural scheme, the brainchild of the boffins of Brussels, which may or may not prove to be of benefit — the set aside programme aimed at reducing the vast over production of farm crops, notably cereals, through the Common Agricultural Policy (CAP) is generally disliked by the majority of farmers, while naturalists have conflicting views on its merits.

157

Having walked over a number of set aside fields in the last year or two, and found them sadly lacking in birds and butterflies, I consider their ecologiaal value to be limited at present.

Even so, I must say that almost anything is preferable, for the wellbeing of birds and mammals — and incidentally to the human eye as well — to a vast expanse of solid, unbroken corn crops or a wasteland of drab plough.

Nonetheless, however beneficial or otherwise such land treatment may prove to be, the present orders from the European Commission, which, as usual our Ministry of Agriculture is trying to enforce too rigidly, that set aside fields must be ploughed up or cut over before the first of July, is quite disastrous for the eggs and young of ground nesting birds, and for the young of hares and roe deer. Such treatment should not under any circumstances, take place between April and August.*

Reverting to those grants and handouts — some time, inevitably, must elapse before they start to produce worthwhile improvements to the landscape, though our flora and fauna must surely begin to benefit more quickly.

Even so, one needs to be of the most sanguine turn of mind not to wonder what is likely to happen in the years ahead, to Suffolk's countryside, and to its wild creatures.

We should be encouraged by the fact that during the past two decades a marked improvement has taken place in people's attitude towards the landscape and its wildlife. Yet, is that attitude firmly based on knowledge and conviction or is it merely uninformed sentiment which can be easily swayed by the media?

One thing is certain, that the English countryside is no longer the haven of peace and quiet that it once was — or that people thought it was. It is becoming more the playground of townspeople who, generally, have no knowledge or

---

* Regulations covering set aside are to be modified for 1994, allowing herbicide spraying instead of ploughing or cut over.

understanding of country ways. Hikers and ramblers invade the fields, lanes and woodlands, trampling on crops and wild flowers and disturbing nesting birds. Other activities such as water skiing, canoeing and motor and motor cycle rallies across country are becoming increasingly popular and all are liable to cause disturbance, if nothing else, to country dwellers, wildbirds and beasts.

Is England to become just one vast garden city with its traditional farmland taken over by huge sports complexes, business parks and fun farms, where children can cuddle young lambs or watch a cow giving birth to its calf. We must, most sincerely hope not.

I began this chapter with a rhetorical question — 'what of the future'? Now, as it nears its end, I must answer that question with another which is — 'who can tell'? Of course that is a fudge, but then it is a brave man who will cheerfully forecast events ten years ahead when even the present agricultural climate is so uncertain.

13

SUFFOLK MAMMALS, BIRDS, BUTTERFLIES AND REPTILES

I have tried, in this memoir to provide an accurate picture of the changes in the Suffolk countryside and in the status of its birds, beasts and butterflies of which I have had personal knowledge during a period of some seventy-five years.

The assessment will I think be helped if we hark back to the years at the end of the last century. Up to that time there had been a number of ornithological works which were really little more than lists of birds shot and birds stuffed, but containing very little information about the countryside as it was in those days or about the numbers and status of its fauna.

The last and most informative work of that century was Dr Churchill Babington's *Catalogue of the Birds of Suffolk (1884-86)*. The Revd Babington lived for many years at Cockfield Rectory, a fine house with an equally fine garden, which I visited quite often in the past, enjoying the thought that perhaps I was sitting in the room in which the learned cleric had produced his magnum opus.

After Babington, there was a gap of nearly forty years until Dr Claud Ticehurst's well-researched *History* appeared in 1932. Ticehurst retired from medical practice in Lowestoft in 1927 when he left Suffolk, though he continued to contribute bird notes to the Suffolk Naturalists' Society's Transactions for a number of years. Copies of his book are now difficult to find as all unsold copies were destroyed by wartime bombing.

Between 1932 and 1950 comparatively little about Suffolk's birds or mammals, is to be found in the literature. The first *Suffolk Bird Report* was put together by Dr N Westall with information supplied by a number of Suffolk naturalists, of whom I was one. I do not recollect that in the two editions of my *Birds of Suffolk*, I made any particular effort to draw attention to bird records of that period. Nor do I think anything much has been written about the status of Suffolk mammals at that time. The emphasise is now all on the present and the future.

Here then is my contribution on the little known past.

SECTION ONE — MAMMALS

Suffolk's pre-1939 population of mammals of practically all kinds was certainly greater than it is today, even though three species of deer — fallow, roe and muntjac, rare or totally absent in those days — are now widespread over most of the county, as of course is that forestry pest, the grey squirrel.

Until the last war there had been a number of deer parks containing fallow deer, as well as a mixed herd of red and fallow deer at Helmingham Hall,but genuine wild deer were rare in Suffolk.

Today there is a considerable number of wild red deer in the Kings Forest, north of Bury St Edmunds, while stragglers are seen from time to time elsewhere in the county. There is also a small herd in Dunwich Forest and recently a group of stags has been reported from woodlands at Langham.

The red deer now living in Breckland forests are said to have an interesting origin. In pre-war days the Norwich Staghounds hunted 'carted deer', some of which had been obtained from Warnham Park in Sussex, long famous for the size and quality of its deer.

When war broke out and hunting had to cease, the hunt,

rather than put down the faithful old hinds which had provided them with so many enjoyable runs, decided to turn them loose in Thetford Forest. In that great wilderness they must have found wild stags to mate with and by the end of the war a small wild herd had become established. It still flourishes and, being of the Warnham strain, now includes some stags carrying particularly fine heads.

Fallow deer, descended from beasts which had escaped from deer parks, notably Ickworth, are now widespread in Suffolk, causing a good deal of damage to crops, orchards and private gardens.

In addition, two other species now occur in the county, the roe deer and the muntjac or water deer. Roe were already living in the Breckland forests before the last war and in the 1950s they began to spread out into Suffolk until there are now very few woodland areas of any size in which roe deer are not to be found.

Muntjac deer, descendants of some which escaped many years ago from Woburn in Bedfordshire, are now established in much of eastern England. The first Suffolk muntjac was recorded in 1940. Others have now colonised much of the county, being particularly numerous on and near the Breck. Apart from man, the muntjac's only enemy is likely to be the fox.

Of Suffolk's other larger mammals, the status of the badger is particularly difficult to define. They are almost certainly more widespread than is generally supposed but being shy, nocturnal creatures that spend the daylight hours underground in well hidden setts, they are seldom seen except by those whose activities take them out and about soon after daybreak.

I have seen only some half dozen badgers in the county during all the years in which I have been about it, though I have handled several that had been killed on the road.

Suffolk foxes are commoner now than they were in prewar days when few occurred in northern and coastal areas; elsewhere they were probably rather uncommon.

Their present range is still somewhat irregular. Local hunts find foxes scarce in places, while in the south-west thirty or more are sometimes culled in a quite small area in some seasons.

Big estates which formerly took pride in always having a

fox in their coverts whenever the hunt visited them, now concentrate on pheasants and foxes are discouraged.

Otters have always lived on Suffolk rivers though probably never in great numbers. In the bad old days they would have had few friends in the countryside. Fishermen, water bailiffs and gamekeepers played their part in persecuting them.

In the 1930s otters were present in small numbers on many of our rivers and the Eastern Counties Otter Hounds found quite regularly on the Rivers Stour and Deben, though they actually killed comparatively few. I went with them from time to time when they visited some river valley with which I was not acquainted. Interesting birds and beasts are often put up when hounds are working.

Otters were also present on the River Glem near my home, and the hunt usually found when they drew the lake in Bridewell Grove at Boxted. Many years ago a friend who had been given the mask of a big dog otter that had been killed at Boxted, asked me to mount it for him. I am no taxidermist, though I have skinned and made up many birds and small mammals during my lifetime. However I had a try and he and I were well pleased with the result. After I had finished it, the head was professionally mounted on the usual wooden shield.

There is no way of knowing now how many otters were living on our Suffolk rivers in those long past days. I seem to remember that the Eastern Counties Hounds expected to kill between twenty and thirty in a season. That would suggest a population of no more than one hundred otters.

They were seldom reported in *Transactions* until after the war.

Sometime in the late 1940s an otter took up residence in a large drainpipe on the stream that flows through Hartest village. It was left in peace there until some young lads set their dogs upon it.

With increasing interest in them, and strict protection by landowners, otters still cling on in some of our rivers, though they are threatened by river pollution and destruction of habitat. Re-introduction in one or two areas seems to be meeting with success. A small cub, and what was probably an adult, were seen a year or two ago by the River Blackbourne at Ixworth and in the spring of 1993, M J Kelly watched one, which he judged to be a young beast, eating a moorhen on the river bank at the bottom of the garden here. Otters seem to be well established on this stretch of the Blackbourne.

That savage predator the mink shows signs of a spread into Suffolk. A number have been killed in the past two years on the Stour at Long Melford. They made their presence known by killing most of the moorhens and wild duck and some young pheasants along a stretch of the river.

Countrymen look upon the hare in widely different ways. For the green coated gentlemen, the harriers and beaglers, it is a most important animal. Farmers regard it in two ways — bad on the farm, good on the table. I think most of us who have lived all our lives with Old Sally, have a secret affection for her.

Farmers and gamekeepers tell me that hare numbers are going up and I hear of over six hundred being shot at a hare drive round Great Barton which is, as we say in Suffolk, 'a tidy lot o' Sallies'. I think hare drives are horrible and avoid them if I can.

There is little need for me to comment on the past and present status of the brown rat, the rabbit and the mole in our countryside. They are always with us in varying numbers and will no doubt remain so.

The hedgehog is a once common creature of our countryside which has suffered seriously from habitat loss and from traffic on the roads. The population of hedgepigs that formerly lived beside our roads — picking up every night a comfortable living from beetles and flies lying dead on the carriageway — has been reduced almost to vanishing point. Most country gardens, and many town gardens as well, used to have good populations of resident hedgehogs. I have only seen two in mine for the past six years.

There can be no doubt that our smaller mammals — the voles and shrews, field mice and harvest mice are infinitely fewer than formerly. This naturally follows the loss of so many rough pastures, copses and hedgebanks in which they made their homes.

In the 1930s, when few Suffolk naturalists seemed interested in small mammals, I began to collect round Hartest a series of all the shrews and voles, and harvest mice, wood mice and yellow-necked mice. The latter were scarcely known then, nor are they now except by competent naturalists. To learn more of their status we shall have to teach our household cats to hand over, without eating them, all wood mice and yellow-necked mice that they catch in winter in our potato stores.

The harvest mouse, once reasonably common, though seldom seen, in Suffolk's cornfields and rough hedges, has certainly become both rare and very local. The huge modern cornfields and the combine harvester between them have removed most of its habitat.

That delightful little rodent is now largely confined to reedbeds and such overgrown hedges as have survived. A few years ago, wishing to obtain a specimen for a museum, I spent one entire day in the only stack yard I could locate in Suffolk, while it was being thrashed out. Rats and house mice ran out, but no harvest mice.

The decrease in rabbits, voles and field mice on which they preyed, has clearly effected the stoat and weasel population. In the 1930s both species were common enough everywhere, even coming into country gardens, and one seldom went out in the fields without seeing one or other of those savage hunters. Nowadays I hardly ever see one, except when I go to Scotland where stoats are common enough. Suffolk gamekeepers also say they see and trap fewer than formerly.

Pollution and the scraping and scouring of our rivers and streams had reduced the numbers of water voles and water shrews very considerably. They were once common enough on rivers and streams; one heard the splash of a diving water rat very frequently as one walked quietly along a riverside.

I have not seen either species on the river at Ixworth, though not long ago I had the pleasure of watching a pair of water voles building a nest beside one of the Ixworth Thorpe ponds. John Wilson says that they still frequent a pond in his garden there. We shall see very few indeed if mink become established

166

on Suffolk waterways.

The red squirrel, once widespread in most of our Suffolk woodlands has disappeared from all except the Breckland fir forests, where it faces little competition from the grey squirrel, an alien species that has spread steadily from the west since the 1950s when the first appeared near Newmarket.

The belief that the grey squirrel actually attacks the red species has never been proved, but it is obvious that our familiar red squirrel cannot live happily alongside the grey family. Despite its engaging ways — we must all have been amused by the television programme *Daylight Robbery* — all foresters and gardeners now regard the American invader as an unmitigated pest.

As dusk fell on any summer's evening in the 1930s, many bats would be flying about over Suffolk's farmyards and village gardens. Pipistrelles were the commonest, roosting under loose tiles and the eaves of houses and particularly wherever old dark lofts and barns offered them shelter. They are still widespread but far less common generally. Two other bat species occurred round about my home at Hartest; long-eared bats, easily recognised by their conspicuously large ears and slow flight, and noctule bats, large, long-winged creatures, that lived in a hollow elm tree just outside the garden. In summer the latter were often on the wing before sundown, flying high overhead as they chased their prey. When their elm tree was cut down, the noctules disappeared. I seldom see one nowadays.

Comparatively little is yet known about the status of our Suffolk bats. They have certainly decreased considerably since the 1930s following the destruction of so many old hollow trees and old farm buildings which used to harbour them.

In the 1950s the Bury Naturalists' Society took active steps to protect a bat roost in chalk caves to the west of Bury St. Edmonds where six species were known to hibernate.

In January 1957 Dr R Stebbings, a noted expert, when leading a party to view the caves, identified twenty-three bats, the majority being Daubentons and Natterers, with a few whiskered and long-eared bats. Subsequent numbers have not been reported.

SECTION TWO — BIRDS

So much for Suffolk's mammals — what of its birds? Sadly, many are also showing a marked decrease when compared with pre-war days. Opinions may differ on the extent of the decrease, but one thing is abundantly clear — the paradoxical situation whereby the common or garden birds, so abundant everywhere in former days, have all declined considerably, while several species that were rare then, or had not nested in the county for a great many years, are now well established as breeding birds, and are even on the increase.

The reason for this is obvious enough. Destruction of so much farm landscape has led to a huge decline in numbers of seed eating and insectivorous birds, while a number of species having different feeding and habitat requirements and that were rare in the past, are now breeding in some numbers and appear to be securely established in man made or man protected habitats.

In the 1930s hundreds of miles of Suffolk's hedges provided food, shelter and nesting sites for a multitude of warblers and finches besides other birds and beasts, as did the old hedgerow trees — many of them hollow — in which little owls, stock doves, tits and green woodpeckers nested in some numbers. I recall how every spring the moaning calls of little owls sounded by day on all sides over the fields surrounding my home, as did the cooing of stock doves which nested commonly wherever there were old tod trees to harbour them.

Whitethroats — hayjacks to the Suffolk countryman — enlivened almost every hedge with their courtship songs and dances. Sedge warblers and reed buntings nested in watery ditches while the characteristic rattling song of the lesser whitethroat sounded from tall hawthorn hedges.

Most of those hedges have now been uprooted or cut almost to the ground, little spring corn is grown and, as a result, most stubblefields are ploughed up soon after harvest and the once familiar clover leys are things of the past. So we no longer see the huge flocks of seed eating birds — linnets, skylarks, tree sparrows, yellowhammers and finches — that once congregated on the winter fields. Not one of those species is anything like as numerous today as it was fifty years ago. Similar decreases have been recorded elsewhere in high farming areas of Britain. As long ago as 1961, a report published by the British Trust of Ornithology on *Population Trends in British Breeding Birds*, showed that once common farmland species had declined by half in the previous ten years. Another more recent census confirmed that those same species had fallen still further in numbers.

My own experience echoes those facts. In 1979, which was the golden jubilee year of the Suffolk Naturalists' Society, of which I have long been a member, I was asked to contribute to its journal a paper on 'Fifty Years of Suffolk Ornithology.' Having consulted my bird diaries, which I have kept assiduously since the age of fourteen, I was able to confirm that up to the year 1939, in the garden of my old home at Hartest or in its near vicinity, forty-nine species were breeding regularly. Fourty years later the number had fallen to thirty. So, in a typical intensively farmed area, nineteen breeding species had been lost over a period of forty years.

As for the status of woodland and semi-woodland species, they seem to be holding up in fair numbers where their habitat has survived, though the nightingale has disappeared from many of its former haunts in the county. In the 1930s a pair nested in one of the shrubberies at my home and we used to delight in watching the parent birds, and later their young, when they came to forage for insects on the lawn. At that period three or four other pairs were nesting in and about Hartest village. None do so now.

Other insectivorous species, all of them summer visitors such as redstarts, common and lesser whitethroats and hirundines, have shown an equally pronounced decrease in population. Their decline has also been hastened by severe and prolonged drought in their wintering area in West Africa, and also by successive summer droughts in Britain when insects have been unusually scarce.

Like their relatives which have managed to survive in what is left of the countryside, garden birds get fewer by the year.

Dare one suggest that modern gardeners are partly to blame, putting too much trust in their horrid sprays and pellets to control greenflies and slugs, instead of leaving it to the thrushes, tits and finches, all of which feed their young on insects, to do the job for them?

In my Ixworth garden, during the past two summers, two broods of spotted flycatchers died in the nest, as did a half fledged cuckoo, all of which appeared to have perished from starvation. That young cuckoo was, incidentally, the first individual I had seen for a great many years, an indication of the fall in the number of cuckoos that has taken place in Suffolk since pre-war days, when young cuckoos were regularly seen in fields and gardens during the autumn.

Until comparatively recent times, when interest in such rural matters seems to have waned, the arrival of the first cuckoo in spring was quite an event among village folk, calling for comment and debate. Mrs Bramble would call over her garden wall to her neighbour Mrs Tussock; 'Do you come out and listen m'dear, here's the fust cuckoo a'callin'.

That harbinger of spring is now becoming quite a rare bird except in a few favoured places, declining in numbers year by year. Perhaps I may usefully repeat here what I wrote about it in 1978, in my *Birds of Suffolk*. In it I said: 'Formerly the cuckoo was a widespread and common summer visitor to all parts of Suffolk, as plentiful in agricultural areas as in woods, fens and heathland. Within the past forty years, however, a very severe decline in numbers has taken place practically everywhere and in only a few scattered locations is it now to be found in anything like its former abundance'.

The cuckoo's song has always delighted me, particularly when heard at 4 a.m. on a June morning as it echoes over our quiet Suffolk fields. The fact that days now go by without sight or sound of that once so familiar bird must distress other naturalists and countryfolk as much as it does me.

Other birds that have shown a particularly marked decline since the 1940s are what might be called the specialised species, birds that frequent only heaths or wetlands. Heathland birds have suffered particularly from the ploughing up of their very limited habitat. Stone curlews and nightjars, tree pipits, stonechats and whinchats have disappeared from many of their former haunts, even within the past twenty years.

A particularly regrettable loss from the list of heathland birds has been the red-backed shrike. It was once widely but thinly spread over the whole county, especially in Breckland and on coastal heaths, and elsewhere in rough uncultivated places, such as railway embankments.

At Hartest we knew it well; in the 1930s a pair bred for several summers in an old bushy meadow just outside our garden. We enjoyed watching the parent birds when they came almost daily into the garden to use the tennis posts as sally points, from which they could catch bees and grasshoppers and the occasional vole. Another pair nested regularly at Boxted Wick. This shrike has not been definitely recorded as a breeding species in Suffolk since 1984.*

The stone curlew, that most typical of wasteland birds, still manages to cling on precariously in the few remaining areas of the old Breckland and is even nesting here and there in the wider forest rides. It has gone entirely from the marginal fields at Culford and Lackford where I found a pair breeding regularly in the 1950s. There was one lone fir tree standing close to Culford Lake, near which a pair of stone curlews nested year after year until the field was ploughed up and the tree cut down. It seems doubtful if there are now more than fifty pairs of stone curlews breeding on the whole of the Suffolk Breck. None have done so on the east Suffolk sandlings for many years.

Apart from the heathland birds, others that have decreased very greatly as a result of their loss of habitat have been the wetland species. So many of our marshes and water meadows in which they formally bred have, during the past twenty years or so, been drained, ploughed and given over to the growing of corn crops or sugar beet.

---

* A pair nested on the Suffolk coast in 1992.

Two species that have suffered particularly are the redshank and the snipe. Few, if any, redshanks are now to be found in summer, breeding as they did in the past, in inland river valleys such as the Deben, Stour and Lark. Fewer redshanks also seem nowadays to nest on our coastal saltings.

As for snipe, their breeding numbers have fallen enormously — as they have done elsewhere in Europe. The *Suffolk Bird Report* could record only nine localities in which snipe had been found breeding in the county in 1991, while the wintering numbers were similarly reduced. The recent drought years, in which essential habitat has dried up completely, have played a significant part in recent decreases but long term loss of traditional habitat has been mainly responsible. Unfortunately, no pre-war records exist of the numbers of snipe then breeding in Suffolk. They must have numbered several hundred pairs.

Certainly, in those days, I knew of at least eight small boggy areas, some no more than half an acre in extent, within a mile or so of my home, where every spring I could expect to find that a pair of snipe had settled in to rear their young. All those sites are now under arable crops.

Yellow wagtails have also disappeared from most of their former breeding haunts following the ploughing up of so many water meadows. In a few places they used also to breed on heather heaths, such as those at Cavenham and Sutton. They no longer do so; most of Sutton Heath was ploughed up years ago. It is not clear why the birds have deserted Cavenham Heath.

It was on such Suffolk heathlands, on both sides of the county, that one or two pairs of Montagu's harriers had struggled to survive, despite heathland fires and harassment by egg collectors and gamekeepers. During the 1920s and 1930s, sporadic nesting took place on the coast, with two successful nests in 1938.

Over on the Breck at least one family party of Montagu's harriers was to be seen every autumn up to the late 1930s, hunting over the marshes alongside the River Ouse at Brandon.

I also saw adult harriers on the Suffolk Breck during the early years of the war. During the 1950s sporadic nesting took place on the coast and probably on the Breck. In 1963 there were two nests in the county; one was in a hayfield near Lakenheath, where the hen sat for six weeks. I then took the eggs under licence, for analysis. They proved to contain no fewer than five different chemicals then in regular use in agriculture, including deildrin.

The last confirmed breeding in Suffolk took place in 1967. I hope we may yet see this delightful harrier returning to Suffolk as a breeding species. At present it is only recorded on passage in spring and autumn.

Habitat loss has also had a marked effect on most of our once common farmland birds. Wartime and post war farming practices, which involved the uprooting of hundreds of miles of hedges and of the old hollow trees, as well as the replacement of ancient farm buildings by draughty concrete structures, left few of the traditional nesting places that had been occupied by barn owls for generations. Modern efforts to provide alternative sites by putting up owl boxes in trees or buildings have, so far, had only limited success.

Meantime, our small population of barn owls continues to suffer from the various pesticides that find their way into the owls' food chain. Others are all too frequently killed by road traffic at night.

Until about the end of the last war, most arable farms in East Anglia supported a varying population of both grey and red-legged partridges, with grey partridges the most plentiful, especially on estates where a gamekeeper was employed to control vermin. Suffolk countrymen and gamekeepers have always maintained that most English partridge broods hatch on Midsummer's Day and a dry, warm week to follow ensures that the young chicks have a good start in life (with satisfactory bags to be made at shoots later in the year).

In those happy days the partridge population was quite high even on unkeepered land where four or five coveys of greys, as well as one or two broods of red-legged partridges, were usually to be found. Alas, all that has changed. There are now many farms in Suffolk where scarcely a single covey is to be found.

The grey partridge, now greatly outnumbered by the sturdier and more omnivorous red-legged bird, does not take kindly to huge, bare fields, early ploughing and constant disturbance by farm vehicles. It misses the winter stubbles and clover leys, and the old traditional meadowland on which it depends for food in the lean months after Christmas. Despite the efforts of those who wish to encourage its return, the English partridge — I prefer to use the traditional name — still shows little real sign of an upturn in numbers.

One species that has probably been lost altogether as a Suffolk breeding bird is the corncrake. My father could remember when corncrakes were widespread and not uncommon in the early years of this century, nesting in hay fields and lucerne crops. The birds were sufficiently plentiful then for village folk to complain that they were kept awake by their loud creaking calls that sounded throughout the livelong night.

Those were the days when hay was cut with a scythe and the man using the scythe had time to see the sitting bird and so avoid cutting over her nest. The introduction of mechanical grasscutters eventually wiped out the entire population of lowland corncrakes, though a small remnant population still clings on in some of the Western Isles of Scotland. Even so, during the 1930s, corncrakes were still being flushed from grass and clover fields during partridge shoots in Suffolk and, less commonly, from corn fields at harvest time.

My last view of a corncrake here in Suffolk was in the autumn of 1939 at Hartest, where I saw three put up, one after the other, out of a field of red clover as it was being cut. It seems unlikely that this curious bird will ever again be found breeding in Suffolk.

To compensate to some extent for the decrease and loses that have taken place since the 1930s among Suffolk's breeding birds, there have been a few increases and quite a number of valuable gains. Two of the most important have been those of the avocet and the marsh harrier. Up to the last war neither of those species had nested successfully in Suffolk for many years, though there had been a number of sporadic attempts by both.

When war broke out in 1939, a considerable amount of deliberate flooding for defence purposes, of marsh and pasture land, took place on the Suffolk coast. The flooding created just the right habitat for the avocet and when it again became possible and safe to visit the flooded areas — some stretches had also been mined — local ornithologists found to their surprise that small numbers of avocets were breeding at Minsmere and on Havergate Island. With strict protection both colonies have flourished, and scattered pairs are also breeding here and there along the coast.

Probably even more important than the return of the avocet has been the re-establishment of the marsh harrier as a Suffolk breeding bird. Greatly enlarged expanses of reedbed in which the bird can nest undisturbed, combined with strict protection by landowners, provide a fine example of conservation success when it is combined with habitat return.

So far as is known, the marsh harrier had not bred successfully in Suffolk for nearly a century, though odd pairs had tried from time to time. Then, in 1945, a nest was found near Lowestoft, from which four young flew safely. In the following years still more pairs nested with varying success. In 1950 there were four nests and during the next thirty years there was a slow but steady tally of young harriers leaving the nest.

According to the Suffolk Naturalists' Society, in 1991, a record thirty-nine nests produced at least ninety-five flying young. A further encouraging sign during the past year or two has been the fact that marsh harriers are starting to nest in non-wetland situations, such as standing corn.

The little ringed plover, another wetland species which also chooses to nest in a dry, stony habitat, though it sometimes does so in corn fields near water, has proved quick to colonise new gravel workings as soon as they become available. The first known breeding in Suffolk took place at Benacre in 1940: now, fifty years later, some forty breeding pairs have been reported at thirteen scattered localities, mostly near the coast.

In pre-war days, two other wetland species, the bearded tit

and the bittern, were breeding in very modest numbers in the reedbeds of coastal Suffolk. In the case of the bearded tit, the increase in its reedland habitat and greater protection of all kinds since the war, has led to a considerable increase in population and a general extension of range. Hard winters nevertheless reduce its numbers to a very low level, as happened in the severe winter of 1947 after which, it was said, only one bearded tit was left alive in Suffolk. Fortunately, the species has the capacity to recover very quickly following mild winters. I remember seeing my first bearded tits on Eastern Broad in 1935.

The bittern had also been showing a modest upturn in numbers during the past three decades. But in 1991, if we are to judge by the number of booming males recorded in three localities, the population seems to have fallen back to about nine pairs, though a booming male does not necessarily indicate the presence of a breeding pair. In any case, mild winters should benefit bitterns and one must hope that their numbers will soon start to increase again.

Of other wetland birds, three species of wild geese have also become well established in the county, all of them being descendants of feral birds from private parks and collections. Before the last war only a small number of Canada geese were kept on estates in north Suffolk, as were some Egyptian geese, both probably colonisers from Holkham Hall in Norfolk. Both are now widespread in East Anglia and appear to be increasing. Greylag geese — also feral birds from captive colonies, have colonised several places in Suffolk.

Some of our native ducks have also increased considerably since the 1940s. Newly flooded gravel pits and reservoirs, such as Alton Water, as well as a considerable number of flight ponds created for shooting purposes, have provided valuable new breeding and feeding habitats for mallard, teal, gadwall and tufted duck. The latter two in particular have increased and extended their breeding areas within recent years.

An interesting post war addition to the list of Suffolk's waterfowl has been the ruddy duck, a native of the New World. This bird of curious habit, behaving more like a grebe than a duck, is now breeding sporadically in the county, having been introduced into the wild in Britain as a result of the escape of captive birds from waterfowl collections. Nowadays, a pair of ruddy ducks may turn up anywhere and settle down to breed on some reedy lake or pond. They are secretive birds at nesting time.

Another species which has become established in Britain since the 1940s, and which is now found breeding commonly throughout Suffolk, is the collared dove. Originally a native of the Near East it began, before the last war, a remarkable westward expansion into Europe and beyond. The first example to be recorded in Suffolk occurred at Lakenheath in 1950.

An important addition to the county's ornithological scene was the discovery in 1967, at a site in north Suffolk, of a flourishing breeding colony of golden orioles, thought to number some eight or nine pairs. It had probably existed for a number of years previously, undiscovered due to the remoteness of the site. It flourished for a time until the habitat was marred by tree felling operations. The colony has now become somewhat dispersed and appears to have fallen in numbers.

The great increase in the numbers of competent observers now living in or visiting Suffolk to watch birds, has established the fact that some species, such as the hobby and the long-eared owl, are more widespread than was formerly believed. It seems probable that at least five pairs of goshawks have also taken up residence recently in our Suffolk forests and are likely to increase.

One other, most undesirable, increase has to be recorded. The magpie, a sharp eyed predator of the deepest dye, destroyer of untold numbers of eggs and young of songbirds as well as gamebirds and ducks, has increased enormously from its low in the 1950s when, like so many other predators, it was suffering from agricultural pesticides. Within the past few years its numbers have increased more than threefold. Although there is now a very efficient method of controlling that avian criminal, too many landowners make too little effort to reduce its numbers.

177

SECTION THREE — BUTTERFLIES

Few flowery lanes, still fewer meadows, all too little common land, old railway tracks bulldozed flat or overgrown with scrub, no red clover or lucerne fields — is it to be wondered at that our Suffolk butterfly population is a mere shadow of its former multitudes?

Butterflies have always been among my lifelong joys. My earliest memories are of holidays spent with my Great Grandmother Golding and Great Aunt Angel who lived at Walsham-le-Willows in what was then called Bridge House, just beside the church. During those Walsham visits I was regularly taken by mother, aunt or nanny for walks down what they called Butterfly Lane. I do not now know where to find that lane, nor even if it still exists, but I can remember quite clearly its clouds of butterflies, especially the multitudes of blues which delighted my childish eyes.

From boyhood I have been an ardent watcher, rearer and collector of butterflies and moths, though my entomological activities have been largely restricted to the fields and woods lying about my old home at Hartest and to occasional days in the New Forest. A green lane, known as Smithbrook Lane, which ran past our house, was my chief hunting ground with its flowery banks, damp verges and great drifts of blackberry and wild rose bushes. In high summer butterflies swarmed throughout its length.

Darney Lane, an old pack horse trail running from Hartest across country almost as far as Whepstead, had even wider flowery verges attractive to still more butterflies. In both those lanes I could expect to see on any fine summer's day more than twenty species of butterflies including, from time to time, such spectacular visitors from overseas as painted ladies and clouded yellows.

Anyone who walks nowadays down either of those lanes — and little now remains of Darney Lane — will be unlikely to see even a dozen kinds of butterfly there and will probably not see a single example of such once plentiful species as the wall butterfly, small copper, skipper or hairstreak. A similar dearth of butterflies occurs over most of Suffolk, though the Breck and parts of the coastal belt still support reasonable numbers.

In a lifetime of butterfly watching I have never seen a fritillary in Suffolk. They have not been recorded here for many years, and the superb purple emperor butterfly seems to be extinct also.

I had not seen the white admiral in our county until a couple of summers ago when I watched a number flying on a sunny day in a great Suffolk wood.

An excellent book, *The Butterflies of Suffolk*, published in 1986, which surveyed the status and range of butterflies throughout the county, does not, I believe, emphasise sufficiently the vast decrease that has taken place since 1940.

SECTION FOUR — REPTILES AND AMPHIBIANS

In general, Suffolk is not noted for the number or variety of its reptiles and amphibians. Adders occur in fair numbers on the Breckland and in other areas of light, sandy soil; so does the grass snake, but the latter appears to shun heavy clay soils, delighting in watery situations on sandy heathland. In the west of the county I have never seen or heard of grass snakes south of Bury St Edmunds, though they may well occur locally in the Stour Valley and elsewhere.

On the other hand, the slow worm is very widespread on heavy land. It is common at Hartest and Somerton and around Long Melford, being particularly fond of churchyards and country gardens. Do grass snakes and slow worms occur together anywhere in Suffolk? At my home at Hartest I often saw slow worms climbing about in the hedges — as a result I had to take care when I was trimming the latter. I have not seen their climbing habits recorded elsewhere. Common lizards are found locally in the sandlings and elsewhere and before the war I knew of a small colony that lived on a roadside bank at Boxted. I think it was destroyed by a road widening operation.

In pre-war days frogs and toads were widespread and very common throughout Suffolk. Their main enemies then were probably foxes, herons, rats and motor cars. In the spring, field and garden ponds everywhere were loud with the croaking of the amorous amphibians. At Hartest, large numbers of frogs and toads congregated from what was evidently quite a considerable distance around the garden to spawn in our two ponds. In some years anything up to one hundred pairs of frogs and toads would be present and their groaning and croaking even kept us awake at night. People passing on the road often commented on the noise they made.

As years went by their numbers dropped steadily and I understand that not more than a dozen pairs appear on those ponds today. I attribute this decrease, at least in part, to heavy road casualties as the toads crossed the road between the orchard and our garden. Similar falls in numbers have been recorded in many places elsewhere. Garden and farm pesticides have, perhaps, been responsible too, but the draining of so many field ponds must also have played a great part in it.

Two species of newt — the great crested and lesser crested — were once common in Suffolk, but the former, a large, handsome creature with a bright orange and black belly, appears to have become rare. The smaller species is still widespread.

I wonder how many people in modern day Suffolk have seen, or would know where to look for a glow worm — which is not, of course, a worm, but a beetle. They were common enough in damp meadows and woodland glades in pre-war Suffolk but ploughing and chemical spraying seems to have reduced them almost to vanishing point. However, I hear that they still occur in good numbers in some of the Breckland forests. They were still to be found also, a few years ago, on an old railway track in west Suffolk. Nearby there was also a colony of roman snails.

SUFFOLK DIALECT WORDS AND EXPRESSIONS

Until at least the end of World War Two, vernacular words and expressions were still in wide use in all Suffolk villages. Some of the words were very local, confined often to a particular group of villages.

Wartime evacuees, radio and television have all combined to dilute the use of dialect words. Now in 1993, most rural young speak basic English, well peppered with Americanisms which they learn from films and television.

Many of the older village folk still use dialect words and converse in what has always been known as 'broad Suffolk'. Presumably the rising generations, living in the villages well diluted with 'foreigners', will gradually shed the old dialect words — and more's the pity.

As a boy and well on into my teens I could, and did converse freely with my rural friends in broad Suffolk.

Here is a list of those words that I remember from the 1930s. Villages to the east of the county probably used a number of words different from those on this list.

I am indebted to F W Pawsey of Cavendish, well known for his amusing talks on the Suffolk dialect, for adding a number of words that were new to me.

General

frawn	frozen
rafty	cold

fare	seems
whooly	really
to pingle	to pick at food
a push	a gathering or boil
a dwile	a duster
dotty	small
botty	conceited
squinny	cross eyed
to twizzle	to tumble over
four deleet	four cross roads
mizzle	light rain
an owd dag	fog or mist
slud	mud
pitman	last of a litter
a rub	a hone, wetstone
sowbug	woodlouse
meece	mice
housen	houses
to hulk	to paunch a rabbit
to hardle	to leg a rabbit
saundy mouse	wood mouse or yellow necked mouse
to cope	to muzzle (ferrets)
a coomb	4 bushels
a rack	a rut
a brew	bank above a ditch
a brorch	hazel peg to hold down thatch
to bop	to duck down
brank	buckwheat
batlins	tree trimmings
shimmaker	cobbler
backhus boy	young handyman
to quackle	to choke
a crome	a fork
staddle stone	mushroom shaped stone to support a stack
dorzled	dizzy

to sussle up — to flush or chase up chickens or pheasants

fleet — shallow

eft — newt

Birds

king harry — goldfinch
stump bird — spotted flycatcher
billy whit — barn owl
willie reeve — stone curlew
red linnet and green linnet — linnet and greenfinch
betty or hedge betty — hedge sparrow
harnser — heron
mavis or mavish — song thrush
merle — blackbird
skritch owl — little owl
olph — bullfinch
puddenpoke — long-tailed tit
titlark — meadow pipit
ground oven bird — willow wren
royston crow — hooded crow